WASTED CALORIES AND RUINED NIGHTS

A Journey Deeper into Dining Hell

JAY RAYNER

ff

FABER & FABER

First published in 2018
by Faber & Faber Ltd
Bloomsbury House
74–77 Great Russell Street
London WC1B 3DA

Typeset by Faber & Faber Ltd
Printed and bound by CPI Group (UK) Ltd, Croydon CR0 4YY

A CIP record for this book
is available from the British Library

ISBN 978–1–7833–5176–3

FSC
www.fsc.org
MIX
Paper from
responsible sources
FSC® C020471

2 4 6 8 10 9 7 5 3 1

Jay Rayner is an award-winning writer, journalist and broadcaster with a fine collection of shirts. He has written on everything from crime and politics, through cinema and theatre to the visual arts, but is best known as the restaurant critic for the *Observer*. For a while he was a sex columnist for *Cosmopolitan*; he also once got himself completely waxed in the name of journalism. He only mentions this because it hurt. Jay is a former Young Journalist of the Year, Critic of the Year and Restaurant Critic of the Year, though not all in the same year. In 2018 he was named Restaurant Writer of the Year in the Fortnum & Mason Food and Drink Awards. Somehow, he has also found time to write four novels and five works of non-fiction. He performs live all over the country, both with his one-man shows and as a pianist with his jazz ensemble, The Jay Rayner Quartet. He is a regular on British television, where he is familiar as a judge on *MasterChef* and, since 2012, has been the chair of BBC Radio 4's food panel show *The Kitchen Cabinet*. He likes pig.

For more information on Jay visit www.jayrayner.co.uk

Contents

Acknowledgements

All of the reviews collected here appeared first in the *Observer Magazine*. I am grateful to Guardian News & Media Limited for granting me the rights to republish them in this collection. I would also like to thank John Mulholland, editor of the *Observer* throughout the period these reviews were published, and Ruaridh Nicoll, who likewise was editor of the *Observer Magazine*, for allowing me to do this fabulous job. I would also like to express my sincere gratitude to the accounts department of Guardian newspapers for reimbursing my expenses so quickly. I literally could not have done it without them. Thanks should also go to my endlessly patient wife, Pat Gordon-Smith, who has to put up with me being out so often, having an awful time.

Finally, as with *My Dining Hell*, my first collection of less than positive reviews, I would like to thank the myriad companions who had to sit through these terrible restaurant experiences with me. As ever, they ate them so you wouldn't have to.

Ruined Nights I'll Never Get Back

Experienced journalists are rarely taken by surprise by the impact of their work. We know exactly what we are doing and why. As I trudged down the marble steps of the Georges Cinq Hotel in Paris, one chilly spring evening in 2017, I knew what I was going to do and I knew what the impact would be. If I claimed otherwise, attempted to feign innocence, I would be lying. OK, I didn't quite anticipate the global reaction. I didn't anticipate the international newspaper headlines and the talking points and the outbreaks of glee.

But if, in the days leading up to the publication of my review of Le Cinq on 9 April 2017, anyone had asked me what I thought the response was going to be, I would have been straight with them. I would have told them it was probably going to be the most read article of my career.

And it was. The review was the most read thing across the entire *Guardian* site for the whole of that Sunday. And for the day after that. And for much of the day after that. An average restaurant review of mine is viewed perhaps 75,000 times and shared some 1,000 times via social media platforms. A popular review will break through 100,000-page views. My review of Le Cinq was viewed about 2.2 million times and shared over 114,000 times. Soon newspapers from New York to Mumbai were writing stories. The high point for me came when the American restaurant blog Eater ran a post headed: 'The Worst Lines of Jay Rayner's Le Cinq Review, With Cats'. It was just that: a series of photos of cats, with speech bubbles filled with quotes from the review. They had attempted to turn me into a meme. I couldn't have been prouder.

Which is what happens when you write an unremittingly negative, 'wipe-the-blood-off-the-walls', 'take-no-prisoners', 'inform-the-next-of-kin' review of a Michelin three-star gastro palace in Paris; one where dinner costs €300 a head. People love it, because people are horrible. You will find it at the end of this collection of pieces about miserable nights I spent in terrible restaurants. If you want to flick straight to it, go right ahead. I won't stop you. Then come back.

The assumption is that I wrote such a brutal piece simply to gain that sort of notoriety. Indeed, many of those who criticised me alleged as much, and obviously I do myself no favours by gloating over the statistics. I can't apologise for that. As I've long said, my job is not to sell restaurants but to sell newspapers (or the digital equivalent thereof). I was just doing my job. Because yes, that review did bring the *Observer* an awful lot of readers and attention. But it had nothing to do with that.

I wrote that review because I was angry: eye-gougingly, bone-crunchingly, teeth-grindingly angry. How bloody dare they? How dare they charge €70 for a starter and €140 for a main course and serve up such a travesty of modern gastronomy? How dare they make cooking of ambition, something I care about (for good or ill), look like a parody of itself? How dare they do this to me and my companion and everybody else in the room? By the time the frozen minced parsley turned up on the dessert, complete with a big 'ta-da!' reveal, my thoughts had turned from what I could do to the restaurant with words, to what I could do to the place with a can of kerosene and a box of matches.

As I say in the piece itself, I didn't go there to have a bad time. I never do. I thought it might be a little absurd, in the way of the grandiose and the haute and the gilded. I knew it would be painfully expensive. (So expensive indeed, that the *Observer* didn't cover all the costs. My companion paid her own bill and I paid half of my own, leaving a 'mere' €150 for the paper to pick up.) But I did at least expect to have a laugh.

In the end the only laughs were the ones my readers had at the restaurant's expense. Because of course, people love negative reviews. As I explained in the introduction to *My Dining Hell*, my first volume of stinkers, originally published as an eBook in 2012, if I had published a collection of my greatest raves, very few people would have bought it. Narratives of positive experiences are cloying and twee and eventually just a little dull and samey. All nice evenings out tend to be nice in similar ways.

But terrible experiences tend to be uniquely terrible. The reader projects themselves into the awfulness, gives thanks that they weren't the one who had to put up with it, and then, like villagers gossiping over the five-bar gate, gorge on all the details. They luxuriate in vicarious displeasure. In the years since that first volume was published I've been accused of revelling in the negative. As a result, I've had cause to count exactly how many of mine really are stinkers. Every year it's roughly the same: a fifth or slightly fewer. Which is to say, ten. The majority, twenty-five, are positive. About fifteen are middling, neither great nor terrible (and therefore the hardest to write). I never go looking for bad restaurants. There are certain big-ticket openings which, like major West End musicals, have to be reviewed. I might have my suspicions about them but I am required to give them the once over. I go to the rest of them because I think they'll be great; often that's because someone else told me so. Alternatively, I'll have studied their website, read the menu and consulted the writings of others, be they blogs or local newspaper reviews. I do my research, specifically to find good places.

But it's the ten negative reviews – the 'utter shitbaggings' as I like to call them – which you remember, isn't it? Of course it is. Because, as I say, you're horrible.

For the first forty-eight hours after the review was published, Le Cinq and its chef Christian Le Squer stayed silent. It made sense. What were they supposed to say? That I was wrong? I would have disagreed with them, but I took it as read that this was what they thought. Eventually, however, the French newspaper *Libération* obtained a quote from that famous spokesperson, 'a source close to' the chef. The review was dismissed as mere 'rich-bashing'.

It was a charge against which I could easily defend myself. In 2008 I had published a book, *The Man Who Ate the World*. It was a journey through seven mega cities, the likes of Moscow, Dubai and New York, in search of the perfect meal. In Paris I decided to do the high-end Super Size Me. In the movie *Super Size Me*, released in 2004, documentary film-maker Morgan Spurlock ate only McDonald's for thirty days in a row to see what the impact would be upon his body. The high-end version I embarked on involved eating in a Parisian Michelin three-star every day for a week: the flagship restaurants of chefs like Guy Savoy and Pierre Gagnaire, renowned dining rooms like Le Grand Véfour, Ledoyen and so on. A couple were terrible, delivering platter after platter of over-processed and over-tortured ingredients. A few were great. They gave you the opportunity to wallow in luxury. One – chef Pascal Barbot's restaurant glorious L'Astrance – was outstanding. I still recall the two fat langoustines in a crystal-clear langoustine broth decorated with single leaves of herbs and purple flowers, like a Monet watercolour; the roasted pigeon with its liver spread on toast; and at the end, a plate of wild strawberries, to which nothing had been done. Because who could improve upon what nature had already perfected?

I didn't begrudge a penny of the three-figure bill. I have long argued that spending large amounts of money on dinner is absolutely fine as long as it's worth it. Some people build their memories from watching their team lose at rugby or from going to the opera. I build mine from meals.

And yet Le Cinq did have a point about me wanting to smash the rich. This collection of stinkers differs a little from the one that came before in that, aside from Le Cinq and a couple of others, the vast majority are in London. They are also from a particular kind of London. A series of taxation policy decisions, which began with the Labour governments of both Tony Blair and Gordon Brown and continued under the Conservative Prime Minister David Cameron, made the British capital especially attractive to a certain type of 'non-domiciled' high net worth individual. They might have been born in Beijing or Moscow or Mumbai, and their money might be in the Cayman Islands, but to all intents and purposes, home is Knightsbridge. They need somewhere to eat. Indeed, they need a whole luxury economy to serve them.

In the years this book covers, that thick, gilded slice of the market came to maturity, encouraging the growth of a particular type of stupidly spendy restaurant, where all sense of value goes out of the window. Consider the revamped Dorchester Grill or the Rib Room of the Jumeirah Tower, Quattro Passi or City Social or an import like Smith & Wollensky. In these places casual dinners at £100 a head or even more became the norm for a particular type of Londoner who, the next morning, would probably not recall what they had eaten. So yes, I did start rich-bashing, and with serious enthusiasm. Because money like that should buy you the sublime not the stupid. Spending money on the good stuff is fine. Throwing it away on the substandard is a particular kind of obscenity. Note the number of times in this collection that I leave before dessert, on the grounds that there's only so much suffering a chap can take. And I really love dessert.

Are they easy targets? Perhaps, but that doesn't make shooting at them wrong. Restaurateurs and chefs who choose to make their money like this need to know it's not OK. Plus, frankly, I am well placed to have a go at lousy places in my own city. Other Londoners don't mind when I lay into the stupidities of the capital. Those of us who live in London know full well there are things wrong with it. For the most part we each of us live in our own particular version of the city. We are quite happy for the failings of the other parts to be pointed out to us and others.

As I've found to my peril, other cities don't respond in the same way. Write a negative review of a restaurant in Liverpool, Manchester or Birmingham and the proud locals will give you a total kicking as a matter of principle, regardless of what they actually think of the place that's been criticised. You'll be dismissed as a metropolitan snob before lunchtime on the day the review was published. Sometimes, frankly, writing a negative review of a place like that is not worth the hassle.

There's another good reason for not writing a negative review. At the risk of sounding pious, anyone doing this job has to be aware of the impact they can have. From time to time I will eat in a small family-run restaurant which is failing: the food isn't anywhere near as good as they think it is or the service is amateurish and, as a result, the tables are empty. The last thing they need is to be taken down by the weight of a national newspaper. In those circumstances I pay the bill myself, chalk it up to experience and move on. The only review in this collection that doesn't quite fit that model is of the Red Duster in the Isle of Wight. But that one was so bizarre, so bonkers and just so weird, I couldn't not write about it. So shoot me.

One element a paperback collection of magazine articles like this will lack is the visual. Each week my reviews are illustrated by terrific full-colour photographs. For the most part I regard that as an added extra. I love great illustrations but it's my job to paint a picture with words. There's only one in this collection where some of those pictures might have added to the experience and that, as it happens, is Le Cinq.

Once I've reviewed a restaurant, I send a list of the dishes I ate to the picture editor of the *Observer Magazine* who then makes contact with the restaurant and arranges to send in a photographer to take pictures of those dishes.

It's very rare that the restaurants are unwilling to oblige. Indeed, it's only happened three times. One was a motorway services (so we ran the piece on the news pages, making even more of their refusal to allow the terrible food to be photographed), one was a brilliant but skanky Sichuan restaurant on the Bethnal Green Road in East London, where the staff's creaky grasp of English meant they didn't have a clue what we were going on about and in any case gave the impression they weren't very interested. The third was Le Cinq. They said their food was far too expensive for them to make it solely for us to photograph. They insisted they would send over their own press shots. The moment I saw a proof of the page ahead of publication I understood why. One of the dishes pictured was an onion gratin which, through a series of different textures including gel balls and purées, was meant to mimic a classic French onion soup. In Le Cinq's picture it was a riot of gold and ambers; a beautiful shimmering thing, like a city on a hill, drenched in sunlight.

In my review I had commented specifically on how terrible the dish looked. What's more I'd taken a photograph of it on my iPhone 7. My picture was of sludgy, sticky, blackness. It was the stuff of depression and gloom. The editors and I agreed that we had to run with the picture Le Cinq had given us. If we did otherwise they might accuse us of actively setting out in some way to sabotage their business. Instead I posted the two photographs (and a few others) side by side on my own website, with a little commentary. We posted a link to that on the online version of review. Then I watched my website crash as hundreds of thousands of people tried to gain access. Personally, I think the words do the job, but if you want to see the compare-and-contrast pictures you'll find them on the 'News' page of my website, jayrayner.co.uk. It's more robust now; it won't fall over.

Otherwise, I hope you enjoy this collection of meals that amounted to just so many wasted calories and ruined nights. At the very least I hope you enjoy reading them a damn sight more than I didn't enjoy experiencing them.

Abuse for the Author

From reviews of the novel *Day of Atonement*, posted to Amazon:

'Terrible book, terrible story.'

'Can only be described as the incoherent ramblings of a self-obsessed ego.'

From reviews of the novel *The Apologist*, posted to Amazon:

'Overthought, self-conscious twaddle. Not worth the money I didn't pay for it.'

'This book was downloaded by mistake. I didn't know how to cancel on Kindle.'

From Twitter:

'Jay Rayner is a good writer but has a face for radio, bless him.'

'Jay Rayner . . . food critic, TV presenter. A face like monkfish genitalia & so ugly it makes you gasp.'

The Legal Small Print

All restaurant reviews are a snapshot of a moment in time and should be understood as such. The date at the top of the review indicates when it was published. Any notes about what may or may not have happened to the restaurant since publication are included at the end of the relevant review. Occasionally, small edits have been made to remove repetitions that would become obvious across a collection like this, or to correct minor inaccuracies not spotted at first publication.

I

High Concepts

Lanes of London
The Marriott Hotel, Park Lane, London, 9 February 2014

Here is a lesson in impotence. It doesn't matter how often I bang on self-importantly in this column about how much I hate menu concepts, how they make me want to stab forks into soft body parts. It doesn't matter if I keep repeating myself. I will still be ignored. They just don't care, these people. And so it is that within minutes of being seated at Lanes of London in the Marriott Hotel by Marble Arch we are approached by a waitress who makes 'suited and booted' look like part of her job description, and she says: 'Can I explain the concept of our menu, today?' Oh God. Clearly it's not: here's a list of dishes, you choose, we bring.

Oh well. I suppose you want to know what that concept is. The Marriott has noticed that street food is now a Thing; that the capital's roads are clogged with reconditioned campervans knocking out stuff that makes sauce dribble down your forearms, some of which is great and a lot of which is stuff in a bap flogged for £6.50. The Marriotts – I want them to sound like an awful dysfunctional couple you once invited round for dinner by mistake – have clearly decided that the only thing wrong with street food is the street bit. Very breezy, streets.

Far better to bring it all inside a room with blaring Now That's What I Call music, windows that appear to have UPVC double-glazing, and bogs that are a country mile's walk away through the Minotaur's labyrinth of a tourist hotel. Hence the menu is divided up between Brick Lane for Indian food, Kingsland Road for Vietnamese, Edgware Road for the Middle East and Portobello Road for burgers and fried chicken because that's all they eat there, poor souls.

There's also a list of haute pub meat dishes, another of fish and a lazy attempt to fob off vegetarians.

As exercises in missing the point go, they don't come much better. The Marriotts haven't just missed the point. They've studied the point, taken a few notes, turned away from it, gone on a long country walk, ended up in a pub, got drunk and woken up in their clothes the next morning with scribbles on scraps of paper from which they have cobbled together a menu.

It's not that all the cooking is truly awful (though some of it redefines the word). It is more that it presents the opportunity to create a meal that makes no sense whatsoever. It's discord fashioned from calories; it's dinner as curated by Stockhausen. Still, at least I now know that Vietnam's pho does not go with an Indian butter chicken. And none of it goes with a limp fattoush salad. No single kitchen can be fluent in all these traditions.

Vietnamese food is not something you can just turn your hand to, like crochet or housebreaking, as their pho proves. It should be a deep bowl of nourishing broth and noodles and beef. Here it comes in small bowls with two tiny, limp pieces of beef sliced as thinly as tissue paper. The beef stock should have a deep, rich flavour. This just makes us mutter about Bovril and think about how good pho on Hackney's Kingsland Road really is.

We then have a long wait. Silly street-food vans with their almost instantaneous service. They don't have leather banquettes for you to sit on so you can study the wine list with its opening price of £28 a bottle while you wait. Eventually our fattoush salad arrives, with not enough deep-fried pitta bread in it and no hit of zesty sumac. Eating this literally three minutes' walk from the Edgware Road while mouthing the word 'Why?' with my mouthful, is an experience that will stay with me.

To be fair the butter chicken from the Brick Lane list is bang on. It's as appallingly over-sweetened and claggy as any version you could find on Brick Lane, where the curries are uniformly dire. Think chicken in tomato soup. The rice is curiously wet, the breads far better. Deep-fried onion rings taste of last week's oil. And whoever wants to dip one in a Marie Rose sauce? I mean it. Who?

There are bizarre inconsistencies. From the 'meat' list, devilled kidneys brings deftly prepared offal, still viscera-pink inside, seared outside. I can't find fault with their cooking. The sauce, however, is bizarre. It tastes of sticky demi-glace and red wine. There's no punch from cayenne pepper at all. They are called devilled for a reason; the cayenne isn't optional.

The Portobello Road section offers the greatest high and the lowest low. The latter is a piece of fried chicken, coated in a bright orange breadcrumb case that flakes off like scabs to reveal pallid-skinned hen underneath. It looks like a boulder that has been badly coloured in by a child. It may be half a very small bird. It's hard to tell. Either way the £12 price tag is outrageous. The honey and sesame dressing next to it tastes of sugar, vinegar and low self-esteem.

But then come their sliders, which are glorious and make me hum happily to myself. They are made from braised brisket, reformed and seared and dressed with a little veal jus, and perched inside tiny brioche buns. Alongside is a pot of pokey horseradish cream plus two hunks of roasted bone, the slippery beads of marrow within topped with breadcrumbs. For £7.90 it's also good value. It's when we eat these that it becomes obvious there are people in this kitchen who can cook, as long as it's from their natural repertoire. Instead they have been smothered by a bloody concept. Did I mention how much I hate concepts?

The kitchen's skills become even more obvious at dessert. Poor Knights of Windsor sounds like a rowdy bunch of mercenaries from *Game of Thrones*. It brings crisp-fried eggy bread with honey-glazed apples, a Calvados ice cream and a jug of custard. Jammy dodgers served in their own cutesy tin are shamelessly crumbly shortbread biscuits sandwiching strawberry mousse with, on the side, a glass of chilled strawberry liquor. These desserts almost banish the memory of the strangeness that has gone before. But not quite.

It's pleasing to imagine the Marriotts might eventually come to their senses. The problem is they've embossed the name of the restaurant into the front step in brass. They came up with a concept. And now they're stuck with it.

What happened next: Given the name really is embossed on the front step it's no surprise there is still a restaurant called Lanes of London inside the Marriott on Park Lane, but it no longer works the street food schtick. Instead, the menu reads like that of a classic urban brasserie. Think steak tartare, club sandwiches, steaks, grills and duck confit. The current dessert menu includes something listed as 'brioche, apple, calvados' which sounds very much like the Poor Knights of Windsor that I so enjoyed.

Pret a Manger
The Strand, London, 23 August 2015

There's a story that in the decades following the Second World War, Reading in Berkshire was regularly judged the most typical town in Britain. As a result, whenever there was a new traffic system that needed trialling – triple anti-clockwise mini-roundabouts, reactive traffic lights, annoying roadside signs with happy or sad faces triggered by your speed – it was introduced first in Reading. Hence, Reading became the most atypical town in Britain. Well, this evening I am sitting in the Reading of the Pret a Manger sandwich shop chain, a branch on London's Strand that has been given every possible bell and whistle for the trial of an evening waiter-service menu and is hence now entirely atypical.

The Pret star outside is black and silver, and there's tiling to match at the far back of the shop. Behind the till a graphic-embossed screen has been pulled down welcoming you to the evening service, and a 'host' stands by the door handing out menus clipped to boards. There are paper place mats, knives and forks – in a Pret! Oh my! – and even guttering candles. It's all rather sweet, like the Year 6s have decided to be really grown up and run a restaurant in Mrs Wilson's art room to raise money for charity. Look! They've printed out menus and everything, bless them.

My companion, flummoxed by the multiple branches nearby, loses her way and is a few minutes late. Orders are taken at the counter and then brought to you. I choose a £25 bottle of prosecco and sit drinking it alone staring out at the office workers hurrying home. These may be among the most depressing ten minutes of my life. It strikes me that going to a branch of Pret a Manger for a classy night out of prosecco drinking is a bit like going to a brothel in search of true love. It could happen but, frankly, we all know it's a victory of hope over expectation.

Don't get me wrong. I like Pret, I really do. It's easy to be down on this sort of high-street brand, but even easier to forget the impact Julian Metcalfe and Sinclair Beecham's chain had on our eating habits from the late eighties onwards. They made good, fresh sandwiches readily available to the masses in a way they weren't before. The mark of a country's food culture doesn't lie in the opening of a restaurant serving Pierre Koffmann's delicate braised pig's trotter, however wonderful it may be. It lies in the national availability of, say, a really good crayfish and mayo sarnie or a quality brownie at a fair price. Some people will regard this as sacrilege; I imagine the comments section below this review online are now like the first fifteen minutes of *Saving Private Ryan*. But that doesn't change the fact: Pret was a game changer in the casual high street lunch market.

Sandwiches, salads and brownies are what they're good at. On the wall is a sign which explains they decided to trial this evening service because their stores are 'often quite busy at lunch but unusually quiet at dinner'. Unusually? There's nothing unusual about that. Nobody wants a sandwich for dinner, unless the evening's gone really badly. And I'm not sure they want this either. Within 100 metres of this Pret there's a Zizzi, a Byron, a Leon and an Itsu, all of which make a better argument for separating you from your cash at this time of day.

Because the food is deeply underwhelming. Much of it

has already been on offer up to six o'clock. Now they can charge you more for putting it on Pret-branded crockery and sprinkling it with chopped parsley. The menu divides between small plates, toasties, salads and 'hot bowls' with a disastrous sideways move into macaroni cheese. Pret's spicy meatballs, at £4.25 for a bunch of tightly packed spheres of indeterminate animal, set the tone by coming in a tooth-achingly sweet sauce. Too much of what we eat comes in a slop like this which has sacrificed grace or interest on the altar of sugar.

A plate of dips tastes like somebody hit the Tesco deli aisle and opened some pots, then went large on the pomegranate seeds. The 'Lebanese' dip is an insult to a whole country. It is red and salty and dull. The 'raita' could come from any number of culinary traditions, being simply yogurt with cucumber. The hummus is nasty, bland, tile grouting.

The hot dishes all come on the same 'quinoa rice', a charmless edible gravel clearly added to everything here to bulk it up. It's there in a completely undressed salad of beetroot, butternut squash and feta. It's there with a horrendously sweet cauliflower and sweet potato curry. Worst of all these is the 'Korean BBQ pulled pork'. Shredded pig wallows miserably in a puddle of gloopy sugary redness, wondering what it did to deserve this. Through the window I can see Kimchee, a Korean restaurant, directly opposite. I dream about being in there. But I'm not. I'm here, at Pret a Manger, trying to have a good night out over an utterly inappropriate bottle of prosecco. As to the kale and cauliflower macaroni cheese, I genuinely do not understand how anybody in the food business can taste that and think it's a good idea. It needs to be put in a burlap sack and drowned in the nearest canal.

So what's OK? The salt beef toastie is OK. It's not brilliant. The salt beef is cut thin and is too lean, but as a whole the sandwich isn't bad, and the caper, rocket and tomato salad on the side is fresh and vibrant. At dessert there's some broken biscuits with popcorn, caramelised nuts and some squirty cream, which I'm sure those Year 6s enjoyed putting together. The best thing is a warmed, squidgy brownie with a scoop of ice cream.

In summary, then, we went to Pret a Manger and had a nice sandwich, a pleasant salad and a toothsome brownie. Which is what we already know they do well. Still, the staff were friendly and engaged. But that makes it only a little sadder. Given the growing sophistication of the mid-market, they have simply under-thought the whole thing. Is it cheap? That sandwich is around £6, and the pulled pork around £7 so no, not really. You'll end up looking at the bill and wondering whether this money could have been better spent. The answer, I'm afraid, is yes, in an awful lot of other places.

What happened next: Very quietly Pret a Manger discontinued the evening service in 2016. Indeed, they did it so quietly that nobody thought to mention it to the team who run their website, until I raised it two years later. Only then did they remove all reference to the experiment from the site. 'We learnt a lot from the

Good Evenings trial and adapted the offering accordingly,' a spokesperson told me. 'We found early on that it was difficult for Pret to run a full-service 'restaurant' and that actually our customers don't expect that from us.' You don't say.

Tapas 37
The Ecclestone Square Hotel, London, 3 April 2016

Ten minutes into our lunch at Tapas 37, the new restaurant inside the Ecclestone Square Hotel in London's Pimlico, the fire alarm went off. It was a vast hacking noise like a goose with bronchitis. Our sweet, eager waitress ran down the narrow dining room flapping her hands while bellowing 'It's just a test' and rolling her eyes with a theatrical shrug, as if to say 'What can you do?' Some might wonder why a hotel which has invested money in a new restaurant, including hiring a chef with some big restaurant action on his CV, would then schedule a fire alarm test for the lunch service. Personally, I can't help but fantasise about how much better a day it would have been for all involved had the fire alarm been real.

I wouldn't wish a fire on anybody's business. But at least if we had been evacuated by a false alarm I wouldn't have had to eat their food. They in turn wouldn't have had to read this review. It would have been a win-win.

The Ecclestone Square Hotel is all shiny and polished

and black and white. It's as I imagine Simon Cowell's hall might be: a touch Athena poster, a touch posh cosmetic surgeon's waiting room. I didn't know whether to order lunch or request Botox. Automatic front doors swish and gasp. Shiny, polished staff brood over the front desk to one side of the hall, while on the other side there's a cocktail lounge with an enormous 3D TV. As I already see in 3D I don't regard this as a boon. We will be the only obvious punters in the hotel for the first ninety minutes, if you don't count the woman who appears to have locked herself in the basement toilet. There seems to be just the one for the entirety of the public spaces. I find my companion outside it, frowning at the door. 'Someone's been in there for more than fifteen minutes,' she hisses at me. 'I tried knocking quietly but a woman squealed. Then she fell silent. Maybe she's dead.'

We decide to cross our legs and retreat upstairs to our table and the eventual ice breaker that is the fire alarm. The website names the new chef, but I won't. Apparently, he has worked with Gordon Ramsay, Jason Atherton and at the world renowned Arzak in Spain. This is not small stuff. It is why I came. Who knows what an Arzak alumnus might be capable of? Now he's here with a menu of tapas, inspired by 'authentic French cuisine' which showcases 'charming little recipes' and is driven by the desire to share 'small French family dishes'. These include Spanish croquettes. There are three on the menu. We choose the chilli cheese and the ham and cheese, and mutter shamefully of Findus crispy pancakes. The waitress says the shrimp croquettes are actually the best, so we order those instead of the cheese and ham.

She doesn't bring them to us. Not that we notice immediately because it takes a while to distinguish between the various fried balls of flavoured béchamel that she has managed to deliver. Eventually we end up with the shrimp ones, too. They all taste nearly the same, varying only on vague back notes of chilli or shrimp. In retrospect they will turn out to be the most edible part of the meal. We will become nostalgic for those darling croquettes.

They're also our introduction to the kitchen's version of tomato ketchup, a gummy condiment full of machismo and casual violence. It is shockingly sweet and acidic and has a texture that usually only comes with the application of industrial emulsifiers, which is remarkable given it must have been made without them. It turns up again in a dish listed as 'tinned sardines'. It is one whole fish, presented in a faux sardine tin, lying on a plank of oily crouton, smeared with a bitter tapenade and more of the tomato stuff. It is meant, I think, to be witty. It looks like something prepared by a desperate *Great British Menu* contestant who didn't quite understand the brief. It looks silly. It tastes worse, a big whack of bitter and salt and sugar and missed opportunities. We leave most of it.

Coquilles Saint Jacques, a single modest-sized scallop for £10.50, looks like a faithful version of the dish. The shellfish should come under a burnished topping of a roux-based sauce with breadcrumbs. Here the sauce had split so that beneath the topping was a watery puddle. It had a lightly bitter back taste. Still, it wasn't as ill-advised as the 'deconstructed' boeuf bourguignon. The centrepiece was a lump of untrimmed short rib, complete with connective tissue where it had clung to the bone. It had clearly been braised a while before, then sliced up and chilled. It had only just about been brought up to warm enough before being glazed. For the lardons, there was a sizable block of exceptionally fatty pork belly, so marble white that I thought at first it was potato. It wobbled as I carved. It was too much fat for me, and that's the first time I have typed those words together. Alongside some button mushrooms were heaps of deep fried breadcrumbs which began to coagulate as the plate chilled. It was, I suppose, a deconstruction of a boeuf bourguignon. It was also the systematic dismantling of all my culinary hopes and dreams.

Next on this menu of small French family dishes: duck spring rolls with bok choi, splattered with another assault by tomato sauce. The spring rolls were thick and heavy and had not spent long in the deep-fat fryer – some of the pastry inside was uncooked. Outside in the hall an industrial strength vacuum cleaner started up because, as we know from the fire alarm episode, at Ecclestone Square housekeeping waits for nothing. Not even lunch in their own restaurant.

The best dish of the day was a slightly overset plug of mango cheesecake with an unadvertised scoop of refreshing blackcurrant sorbet. The three rectangles of pastry in a chocolate and pear mille-feuille were dry, tired and under-sweetened. The two lumps of pear were completely unripe. They were hard to the edge of my knife. And that detail sums up the place. Why would an experienced chef, one with time at Arzak on his CV, choose to serve an unripe pear? It baffles me. But not quite as much as the £120 bill we were presented with. Come, friendly fire alarms.

What happened next: The Ecclestone Square Hotel closed Tapas 37 in 2017. They now run a straightforward brasserie.

Studio 88
London, 25 March 2018

Booking a table at Studio 88, a new live music bar near Leicester Square, central London, where almost all the food is served in cones, took two attempts, seven phone calls, a cancelled booking (because they'd forgotten it was press night and my pseudonym barred me entry), a bunch of emails with fifteen terms and conditions ('While we welcome pre-wedding parties, we cannot accept any paraphernalia') and a £50 charge to a credit card. We were warned to bring picture ID.

I said: 'But I'm fifty-one.'

They said: 'No exceptions.'

After all that effort, we had to go. It's on a side street. You'll know it by the cordoned-off queue, waiting to be taken through a metal detector, for their ID to be scanned and their faces photographed. I also got frisked. I can't lie. If there's one thing that really encourages the appetite, it's being felt up by a total stranger with meaty hands. Apparently, all of this is a requirement under a late licence from Westminster council – though why any-one would willingly run a business that involves setting up what feels like a small Eastern European state at the height of the Cold War beats me.

Down the stairs, past the cloakroom – £2 an item – and you're into a nightclub space with video walls of exploding fireworks, back-lit bars and a low stage with two baby grand-shaped digital pianos, attended by two young chaps fondly murdering Adele's back catalogue. We are shown to our table, graced by two champagne flutes. But this being under Westminster council's licensing laws, they are crafted from beauti-fully moulded plastic. Likewise, when we order a bottle of wine it arrives pre-decanted into a plastic carafe that has gone that cloudy colour from a few too many runs through the dishwasher.

The plastic flutes are filled with cheap prosecco. This is part of the deal. Or as the T&Cs put it: 'Each of your guests is required to have our set menu, which includes two small cones, two large cones, a side cone, dessert and a glass of prosecco for £25.' So, it's less dinner, and more of a contraflow on the A1 just past Scotch Corner.

We'll come back to that food. I have to talk about it, to ease the pain more than anything else. But it would be utterly disingenuous of me to continue like this with-out getting to the nub of it, which is to say: Studio 88 is brilliant. I'd go back in a heartbeat. Yes, getting into the place is a Kafkaesque nightmare. And yes, the food is that killer combination of appalling ideas and dreadful execution. But at 8 p.m., those two pianists are joined on stage by a gang of other musicians to form one of the tightest house bands I've seen in years. And I've just come back from New Orleans, where every damn bar has one.

Armed with the GuitarTabs app, and a serious repertoire, they took requests and executed each one with wit and precision. Sometimes it required whichever pianist was leading the band to call the chord changes through the song, but they didn't break sweat. From Stevie Wonder to Chaka Khan, 'Uptown Funk' to 'Valerie', Queen to Macy Gray, they killed it. And credit, too, to the management, which clearly recognises that musicians like this cannot be flogged to death. Four pianists worked the keys when we were there, in shifts.

Likewise, the service is terrific. Managing table service cheerfully when 80 per cent of the room is on their feet dancing, as they were from about 8.10 p.m., is not easy. This lot managed it with grace and professionalism. What's more, they had to do so in the face of adversity, which is to say, the notion that putting food in paper cones, placed in spindly holders, is a good one. It isn't. Each time they served us with a cone they made a point of putting it directly into our hands.

It took me a while to work out why. If they put them on the table they would invariably fall over, as the only one they placed down did, spilling its contents. Sadly, they replaced it, which meant we got to try their take on salmon tartare. It involved avocado, olives, currants, coconut and despair. Mine. If someone had made this for me at 3 a.m. from what was lurking at the back of the fridge, I'd have understood. But to pay someone to do it seemed to me like a terrible error of judgement.

What's amazing is that it wasn't the worst thing we were served. There was the sticky, gelatinous vegetable summer roll in its coagulating rice dough overcoat, which my companion said felt like 'holding a flaccid penis'. (There are certain things that, once said, cannot be unsaid.) There was a cone full of quinoa gravel, burying the tiniest fragments of meat, which the menu told me was miso-glazed pork with black beans and spicy coconut yogurt. Without that seemingly random assemblage of words, I wouldn't have known. It was a debris through which you had to pick in search of survivors. Sadly, there weren't any.

Crab croquettes were mostly potato and had a 'Mum's gone to Iceland because she hates me' quality. They were served completely tepid, which is unsurprising given they were in a paper cone. The worst of these tepid dishes was an extra sharing platter of dim sum at a shocking £20, which reminded me of those sold in a well-known Asian supermarket chain. They'd been allowed to cool and coagulate until they were stuck to the slate they had been served on. Maybe they were trying to save us from eating them. We pushed the slate aside and leapt up to dance to 'Don't Stop Me Now'.

I know what you're thinking: what exactly did I

expect? It's a dance bar off Leicester Square. Of course the food is going to be a disaster of a calamity of a travesty. Except that my experience at Albert's Schloss in Manchester recently taught me never to make assumptions. There, the superb live music was matched by the cracking food. Why shouldn't Studio 88 be the same? Surely it's in my favour that I travel so damn hopefully.

None of this lousy cooking detracts from the things Studio 88 does well. The band are superb. The staff are great. I really would go back. Just don't make me eat anything.

What happened next: Within days of the review's publication I was emailed by Alan Lorrimer, who owns Studio 88. He told me he had enjoyed reading the review and went on to say he totally agreed with me about the licensing terms they had inherited. It was clearly driving him nuts, but there was little he could do about it. The dance bar is extremely popular, especially at weekends. For now, the 'cones' menu remains in place, though Lorrimer said he was reviewing the situation.

Circus
London, 26 June 2011

We had been at Circus a short while and had only just received our food – I use the term loosely – when a young woman in black bra, hot pants and fishnets came and danced by our table, with flames burning upon copper dishes laid upon her upheld palms. If only she'd tripped and set fire to the curtains. Apart from the fact that we might briefly have been able to glimpse what was on our plates through the Stygian gloom – what exactly were these ingredients, and what had they died of? – it would have brought the evening to an early close, which would have been a relief all round.

To be honest I was predisposed to hate Circus before a single piece of food had arrived. Then again sometimes taking an instant dislike to something can save time. It wasn't just that they did not return my phone call requesting a table – I'm waiting still – or that, booking online, they demanded a credit-card number. There was also the less-than-charming announcement as we arrived that we had to give the table back in two hours. Maybe the receptionists had tried the food and were trying to be kind.

It is not the concept of Circus I dislike. Dinner and a show is a great idea. You just have to do both bits well; here neither part of the equation works. This is not to reflect badly upon the performers, who give it their all, or would do if they were given enough time and space in which to do so. But Circus is a messy compromise, built around the need to keep moving the punters in and out, to keep hosing them down with over-sugary cocktails – think type 2 diabetes in a glass – and pelting them with over-priced platefuls of what might make great props in a freak show but, here, pass for main courses. The room is simply too small for the promise of the name to be realised.

During our meal, there was a chap who dangled gymnastically from a fold of cloth above the wide central table which doubles as a stage, while trying to keep his feet out of the salads, followed by the dancing girls with the flaming palms. There was also a woman who stripped rather briskly down to polka-dot pants and bra before removing the latter to reveal tasselled nipples. My companion had to take my word on this. A waiter obscured her view, while delivering main courses nobody could possibly have wanted. 'Look,' my friend said, 'if someone's going to get their kit off the least she deserves is people being able to see.' The upside of the four-minute performances is that when they start, shutters come down on the kitchen hatches, meaning that for a while no food can be delivered.

Ah yes, the food. Sticky concoctions, summoned from the gates of hell, or the kitchen, whichever is closer. It's the kind of thing you'd get at a Harvester, only with less subtlety and more cynicism. A sharing plate to start brought crappy deep-fried squid, really crappy chicken satay skewers with a sauce that made the word 'suppurate' dance across my mind, a truly crappy hoisin duck salad, which amounted to hard, dry bits of meat hiding in a hedge, and astonishingly crappy deep-fried beef pasties. They used the word 'empañadas' to describe these; I would use words that aren't allowed in a family newspaper.

The main courses both cost me around £23 and my innocence. Hard, dry duck confit laid on overcooked peas and mint in a sickly-sweet Thai red curry sauce isn't just a bad idea or bad cooking. It's also really bad manners. Large scallops and prawns were grotesquely over-seasoned and served with a saffron and sour cream sauce that had the authentic tang of something with which you'd clean a bathroom sink in an attempt to hide bad smells. With the side dish of jalapeño onion rings, we were back thinking about a Harvester and wishing we'd gone to one of those instead.

On the grounds that we'd suffered and spent enough, we decided to forgo dessert. In any case our time slot was up, though our waitress invited us to wait and watch the next act, a camp Elvis impersonator with lots of gold hula hoops, bigging up the gay subtext to 'Jailhouse Rock'. He was good. And that's what is most depressing about the whole business. The staff really are doing their damnedest. They are giving it their all. They are friendly and charming and attentive. And they are also completely and utterly wasted.

What happened next: The sickly-sweet, quasi American menu has been entirely replaced by a Pan-Asian affair, with emphasis on Japan – think sushi, sashimi and gyoza – overseen by an experienced executive chef called Andrew Lassetter. Circus has traded very happily since this review, and has overwhelmingly positive customer feedback on both Time Out London *and* Google.

2

Lost at Sea

Lands End at Sunborn
Royal Victoria Dock, London, 1 March 2015

In naming this week's restaurant Lands End, the operators of Sunborn London, the superyacht hotel which houses it, were almost right. It is indeed the end, though not of land. It is the end of hope, of good taste, of ingredients which deserved so much better. Generally, bad places have a redeeming feature or two: a dish that passed muster, a sauce that made sense. The meal served aboard the Sunborn was remarkable for having not a single one. That old gag about stopping for chips on the way home? It is no longer a gag. That's exactly what I did. There was a burger, too. I was hungry.

Some will regard this as a cheap shot. We all know you shouldn't eat in restaurants that boast about the view, that rotate, or sit on water. It will never be about the food. It will always be about the view or the rotating or the water. But this one looked different. From the outside the Sunborn, moored by the ExCeL exhibition centre in east London, looks like a gargantuan torpedo; it is every high-end, high-polished white kitchen appliance you've ever perved over, its lights twinkling prettily off the oily waters of the Thames. It's a greased Kanye West music video waiting to happen. Who wouldn't want a go on that?

And then there was the menu. It wasn't poetry, but it had a pleasing narrative thrust. It mentioned coriander shoots and salt-baked beetroot. There were porcini ravioli with the beef cheek and cornichons with the duck rillettes. It listed enthusiastic prices: starters at £12, mains at £25 or even £30. If they were charging that sort of money it should at least be adequate? Adequate, aboard a superyacht that looked like the setting for a Kanye West video, could be loads of fun. Couldn't it? In this I am an idiot; a sweet and trusting one, but an idiot all the same. Mind you, my failings are as nothing against theirs.

We embark via a lift that opens from the quay. It takes us up two floors and back thirty-two years to 1983, when all metalwork was fake gold, all staircases swirled upwards in big curves, glass panels were etched with images of ferns and carpets looked like someone had thrown up on them. It looks like late Elizabeth Taylor realised as interior design.

Up those stairs is a reception desk, above which a faulty light bulb flickers in a way news anchors have to warn epileptics about before screening reports containing flash photography. Beyond that lies a dining room that makes the foyer look classy and subtle. Almost everything here is clad in shiny brass-coloured planks, including the ceiling. I like my own image as much as the next narcissist but this is ridiculous: it means the terrible time I am about to have will be reflected back at me from every surface. The waiters, who for the most part do a valiant job in terrible circumstances, wear name badges, unreadable in the shimmering gloom. For this they should give thanks.

And so it begins. A bottle of water is warm. Bread rolls look like they arrived in the kitchen part baked, and in need only of finishing – in which case the kitchen failed at their one job. They are undercooked. Garlic butter tastes old and slightly rancid. No matter, there will be starters. Eventually. The only thing that can make bad food worse is being forced to wait for it. We have enough time in which to all but finish a bottle of Albarino, one that can be found on wine lists all over London at no more than £30 and here costs £39.

The alcohol doesn't blunt the pain. A black pudding cake, looking like an emotionally neglected hockey puck, arrives under a glass cloche. It is removed and a moat of gluey chive and mustard velouté is poured on. To say it tastes watery is an insult to a chilled glass of water (something they cannot manage here). It is a sludge of nothing. The black pudding cake is hard and compacted and tastes mostly of salt. It is carelessness and disregard, fashioned out of wasted calories. Citrus-cured salmon gravadlax with daikon, pickled cucumber, watercress and yuzu, brings half a dozen small cubes of salmon that taste of malt vinegar, and an £11 addition to the bill.

The half-eaten plates are cleared. We are not asked why they are half-eaten. That would be intruding on private grief. Time stretches out, restlessly. We are brought warm glasses of pinot grigio to apologise for the long wait. By now the main courses feel less like a promise than a threat. It turns out not to be an empty one.

The thinnest piece of turbot arrives so over-cooked it crumbles on to dry, distressed borlotti beans. There are tangles of chewy meat which the menu says are bits of ham hock, and more of the rancid butter from a beurre noisette that has solidified on the plate. It's a dish in need of antidepressants. Arguably, my beef cheek is worse. It is hard and solid. It looks like a growth of the sort that might feature on a Channel 5 programme about embarrassing medical conditions. The tumour sweats under a blanket of sticky, over-reduced sauce that has the brutal hit of Marmite. Porcini ravioli are undercooked, leaving the pasta hard. A side dish of sautéed mushrooms tastes of raw garlic, salt and hypertension.

This food isn't just poor compared, say, to a roast swan I had the other week. It isn't me being snooty and prissy and overly demanding. It is a blistering display of incompetence; of cack-handedness and cynicism and bad taste. My companion asks if we have to stay for dessert and I agree that we don't. Even utter perfection fashioned from salted caramel could not save this evening. Over barely touched plates I ask for the bill. Our waitress notices the debris. She asks if there is something wrong with the food. I give it to her straight. Something wrong? Nothing is right. She comps the bottle of wine.

Outside, a perfect evening is capped by threats of casual violence from a man who accosts us with stories of having been arrested and who now wants money. We shake him off and get into a cab. I give the driver directions to the burger place we need; and with relief, we head towards a place where I know the food will not hurt us.

What happened next: Not much, to be fair. The menu has changed very little, and currently includes a 6oz fillet steak for £36. The various customer review sites all award it four out of five stars. That said, in September 2017 the Daily Mail *sent their self-styled anonymous 'Inspector' to give it the once over. He criticised the prices, the 'faux poshness', the slow service and awarded it one star out of five.*

The Red Duster
Isle of Wight, 23 September 2012

Words never fail me, but occasionally the will does. Sometimes when dinner has let me down, I close my eyes and try to find my happy place, the one with all the food that makes sense in it. For a few days after eating at the Red Duster in Cowes I struggled with how I was going to write about it. I considered bigging it up as a work of postmodern genius, a culinary game to rank alongside the moment in Mike Leigh's film *Life Is Sweet* when budding chef Timothy Spall declares his new menu will include black pudding and Camembert soup, liver in lager and pork cyst. I quickly realised that would be tiresome. Anyway, the kitchen at the Red Duster thinks it's OK to sauté potatoes in Marmite. In the face of that, whimsy and satire scribble a despondent letter of resignation, and leg it.

The Red Duster looks like a cross between a bordello and a Torquay guest house. There are fountains of red napkin exploding from the glassware, church pews to perch on and on the walls, paper embossed with a leaf pattern in scarlet. No need to look at that for too long, for the menu descriptions are there to distract you. I especially liked the cannelloni made with 'basil-enthused pasta'. How does one enthuse pasta exactly? Do the chefs run around the kitchen tickling the dough with fronds of the stuff, shouting: 'Cheer up, mate, it might never happen'?

My sauté of chicken liver and bacon 'satay' was no less bonkers. Chicken livers. Peanut butter. And bacon. Believe me. However hard you try, nothing good could ever come of that, and nothing did. It was a mess of something dark and heartbroken. Duck & Waffle, which I reviewed a few weeks back, served drunk food; this is food for drunks whose partners have abandoned them, leaving them with an almost empty fridge. By comparison the hot smoked mackerel on a rhubarb and ginger relish sounded relatively sane. The brilliance here lay in the kitchen's ability to flatten the fillet's skin and stamp it with creases of the sort you normally only find in the shop-bought vacuum-packed kind. It came with two equally industrial-looking slices of brown bread and an under-sweetened mess of rhubarb.

Onwards. Reasonably well-cooked fillets of sea bass came swaddled in a deadening blanket of unseasoned over-reduced cream. Alongside them were 'laver bread croutes', which is what happens when you put that Welsh seaweed mush between two greased pieces of bread and into a Breville sandwich maker. Sweet and sharp chocolate-brushed duck – a version of which genuinely was on Timothy Spall's menu – brought chewy animal cooked to the grey of a winter seascape. It tasted of the sweet counter at WH Smith. The roasted sweet potatoes and butternut squash didn't really help. At least there was the distraction of those potatoes sautéed in Marmite, in a puddle of fat so deep you could measure it with an engine dipstick. Oh God. Never again.

The red velvet and cherry mille-feuille, a take on Black Forest gateau, stood out for being sensible and reasonably well executed. It was sweet; it was 'bring me my insulin' sweet. But that's not necessarily a failing. Our other dessert, the vanilla chocolate-box surprise, sounded like a full-colour spread from the politically incorrect pages of *Razzle*, circa 1983. Never order anything with the word 'surprise' in the title. Here the surprise was that, if you don't know what you're doing, you can turn what's meant to be a chocolate torte into something with the consistency of hard, cold butter.

If any of this was dirt cheap it might not have mattered, but it wasn't. Main courses are in the high teens, with some topping £25. Service, by a sweet young couple, is kind and efficient. It really wasn't their fault they had to bring us all the things we had to eat. Or didn't, as the case may be.

What happened next: Mostly a series of emails from the yachting fraternity who told me they always stopped off at the Red Duster during Cowes week, the famous sailing regatta, and that they rather liked it. They did, however, acknowledge eccentricities. The current website has the words 'Marvellous Marmite' on the home page, although the famed potatoes in Marmite are no longer listed on the menu and nor is the 'basil-enthused pasta'. What a shame. It now reads like that of a normal restaurant – seafood chowder or Waldorf salad to start, a rib eye or roasted salmon for mains – which may explain the five-star ratings on most review sites.

Fancy Crab
London, 27 August 2017

Eating crab, like building kitchen extensions and sex, is very messy when done properly. You have to roll up your sleeves and abandon yourself to the mucky business at hand, with hammer, crackers and pick. The white meat must be hard won, the brown meat scooped from nooks and crannies. I've always thought of it as being akin to that myth about eating celery: that you burn as many calories breaking the bastard down as you gain from the seafood with which you are rewarded.

Fancy Crab, which sounds like an unnecessarily extravagant yoga position, is designed to take the mess out of crab, which is like trying to take the rum out of a mojito or the meaning out of life. It's a crab restaurant for recently married couples who hope they'll get divorced before they ever reach the companionable stage in which one of them brushes their teeth while the other has a pee. It's an extraordinarily expensive way to wonder about the point of it all. You could get the same effect for free by staying home and watching *Love Island*.

The restaurant's shtick is the enormous red king crabs, fished from the cold waters of the North Pacific around Alaska, which can grow to be five feet across, and have legs like Arnold Schwarzenegger in his prime. The leg meat is the whole point. It is meant to be the sweetest and the best, the Bugatti of the shellfish world. At the start of the meal our waiter, who is by far the best thing here, brings out a whole king crab on ice for us to look at, its legs curled under. When confronted by these at Beast, still alive in tanks and backlit in icy blue, I was reminded of the facehugger in *Alien*. Now I recall the scene from Douglas Adams in *Restaurant at the End of the Universe* in which a genetically modified cow is brought out to the table still alive, so it can recommend its own primest cuts.

Let me dial down the snark for a moment. I can see the point of a restaurant dedicated entirely to one glorious ingredient. I can admire the way the menu goes all in. Sure, there's a steak for the shmuck in your group who didn't quite understand the point of the outing. They have some oysters. But for the most part it really is all about king crab. They've put effort into the decor, from the huge blow-up of a king crab on one wall to the way the beast has been subtly included in other works of art, in a *Where's Wally?* sort of way. There are bare brick walls and high ceilings and those lovely waiters wear real bow ties, which they had to learn to tie from YouTube videos. Obviously you know it's going to be nose-bleedingly expensive. That doesn't mean it can't also be good.

Fancy Crab isn't good. It's a terrible waste of their money and our money and everybody's time. It starts with the smallest thing. A plate with two warmed bread rolls, dull and springy, come with discs of seaweed butter. They have been dredged carelessly from a bowl of iced water. Accordingly, there is a puddle of cold water all over the plate, soaking into the rolls. The butter is unsalted and, like me, tastes only of cold, hard fat. A wine waiter doesn't take our order until just before the starters arrive, and returns with entirely the wrong bottle, a massive red. The starters are half finished before the correct bottle of Spanish white at an excruciating £40 turns up.

A 'tempura' crab claw costs £12 and isn't. Tempura refers to a particular kind of lacy batter. These look like inflated versions of the ones you can buy at Iceland for pennies and come coated in exactly the same sort of DayGlo orange breadcrumb shell. Three bites and it is gone. An accompanying 'chipotle' mayo tastes like Marie Rose sauce. There is no heat. The crab is also offered cold on ice, or grilled. We go for a leg cut of the former, the shell already sliced through so there is no effort getting at the meat: £24 worth disappears in about ninety seconds. A squid ink mayo is salty and blunt. A mango dip is fruitier and rather pleasing.

Outside of eating it cold with mayo, Singapore chilli crab is one of the very best dishes using both meat and shell ever invented. It should be salty and sweet and spicy. Eating it should get sauce on your ear lobes and sweat on your brow, and a massive burst of endorphins into your bloodstream as your body recovers from the burn. So surely, how much better if it's made with this king of all crabs? Here it costs £34, which does rather encourage expectations. It's a slippery, sugary mess, with no heat at all. This is because they serve chopped red chilli on the side. It's like serving pork belly without the fat, or smoked salmon without the smoke. It's missing the point entirely. There's also a sugary, toasted sesame seed bun of the sort burgers come in at Byron. The sweet notes continue in a sashimi of sea bass. The knife work is good, but the dressing is all sugar and carelessness and a shrugged teenage 'whatever'. It only gets finished out of hunger.

Chips come doused in truffle oil, are tepid and remain unfinished; a garden salad is dressed well enough but contains fridge-cold slabs of tomato that taste of nothing. The desserts include something called 'king crab' cheesecake, which obviously has to be ordered. It's a loose oblong of crushed biscuit base, topped with a foamy vanilla cream sprinkled with pink stuff to make it look like a king crab leg. Which is, I suppose, better than a cheesecake that actually tastes of king crab. The best dish of the night is a luscious salt caramel ice cream with a perfectly serviceable chocolate fondant. It's nothing special. It just manages not to be actively offensive.

Who is Fancy Crab for? I have no idea. It occupies a stretch of London's Wigmore Street crowded with shops selling stupidly expensive kitchens to people who probably don't cook. It feels of a piece with that. It's a restaurant predicated on one idea: that a single really expensive ingredient will make your life better. I'm sorry to be the one to tell you this, but it won't.

What happened next: The restaurant continues to trade and while dishes have been added to the menu – you can now get a 'deluxe' seafood platter to share for £100 – it is still the same concept. A few months after this review, there was another in the Daily Express *by the grandly bylined Lady Barbara Judge. She said she liked it very much and complimented the crabs for being 'red and white and huge'. She liked it so much she went twice.*

Smith & Wollensky
London, 12 July 2015

Cooking a steak well is tricky, because you cannot see inside the meat. It takes experience and knowledge. Cooking chips is easy: use the right potatoes, give them a couple of runs through the hot oil, make sure they're the right colour, perhaps even taste a couple. The job is done. At Smith & Wollensky, the new London outpost of a well-known small American steakhouse chain, we sent back the chips because they were tepid and under-cooked. They returned to us hot and undercooked. And in that one example of carelessness and lack of attention to detail, you know all you need to.

But I had to sit through the whole damn meal so I don't see why you shouldn't, too. This US business has swaggered into London like it thinks it's the bollocks. The description is almost right, if you remove the definite article before the reference to testicles. It is about as shoddy an operation in separating people from inexcusable amounts of their cash as I have seen in a very long time.

But first a little context. Until about a decade ago Britain was crying out for a proper steakhouse on the American model; one that knew how to source beef, cut steaks thick enough and char them properly. Endless feeble attempts came and went. Then we got both Goodman and Hawksmoor, the latter adopting all the tropes of the US steakhouse, but giving them a pronounced British accent. It put prime cuts of British beef centre stage.

And now comes Smith & Wollensky (hereafter S&W), which bellows loudly about importing US Department of Agriculture beef from Iowa, but which is backed by a consortium from Ireland, a country which produces some of the best beef in the world. They have spent a reputed €10 million, and you can see where every cent has gone. The conversion of the basement and ground floor space of the 1930s New York pastiche Adelphi Building just behind the Strand is an orgy of leather and wood, of brass rail and tasteful mural. It can seat 300 people. Across fourteen services a week I calculate they will need to find roughly 4,000 people able to pay the prices required to return that investment.

Cocktails are £13. That buys me an insipid Moscow Mule served in a stupid brass mug with a thin plastic straw. Five pleasant enough medium-sized seared scallops with shards of crisp bacon are £18; four jumbo prawns are £14. Except they don't call them prawns, because despite the London setting the place must have a transatlantic drawl. So prawns are shrimps and all steaks are listed in imperial measurements. The USDA cuts include a 24oz bone-in ribeye and a 21oz sirloin. The prices for these are astonishing. The former is £65, the latter £62. To put this in context, at Hawksmoor the bone-in sirloin is £5.60 per 100g. At S&W it's £10.42 per 100g.

Is that simply because it has travelled? Not if the fillet steak prices are anything to go by, because S&W have sourced those from the UK. At Hawksmoor fillet is £11.33 per 100g; at S&W it's £14.55. Both the menu blurb and the waiting staff bang on about this being the best steak you will ever have. The menu also mentions a list of blackboard specials – T-bones and so on – all of which have run out by 8.20 p.m. We order the bone-in ribeye. The char is feeble and the overwhelming taste is of salt. Worse is the texture. It's floppy. Part of this, I think, is a cultural difference; Americans like to celebrate steaks based on tenderness, as if being able to cut a piece of dead animal with a butter knife is an aspiration. I think that if you're going to eat beef, you want to know it has come from an animal that has moved. This steak slips down like something that has spent its life chained to a radiator in the basement.

The sauces are dire. A béarnaise is an insult to the name, lacking any acidity or the anise burst of tarragon. An au poivre sauce is just a shot of hot demi-glace. A side salad is crisp and well dressed. We take comfort in it. Many other sides are priced for two which is a quick route to higher profit margins and greater food waste. The £9 battered onion rings are good; the £10 truffled mac and cheese is dry and tastes not at all of truffle. Those terrible chips come in the kind of mini-chip-fat-fryer-basket used at chain pubs.

Service is omnipresent. Twice we ask to keep our bread and side plates when they attempt to remove them. When a third waiter lunges in I finally admit defeat. Take them if you're so bloody desperate. How hard is it to communicate a table's wishes to the half dozen people working a corner of the floor, especially when a meal is going to cost more than £100 a head?

Our waitress, an escapee from Hawksmoor, is lovely – efficient, charming and utterly wasted here. She has been sent out on to the floor in a jacket she admits is about three sizes too large for her and is already stained. Either the management gives a damn about the dignity of its staff or it really doesn't. Still, she speaks fluent Smith & Wollensky, intoning the oft-repeated figure that theirs are the best 2 per cent of all USDA steaks. God help the other 98 per cent. We try to love it, really we do, but we just can't. Clearly the poor animal died twice: once in the slaughter house, once on the grill. We give up and hope she doesn't look too distraught. Curiously, the menu announces in small print that items 'may' be cooked to order. May? Only may? Don't put yourself out, guys.

We finish with the 'gigantic chocolate cake' which costs £15. It comes with a mini milk urn full of chilled, lightly whipped and sweetened cream. That cream is by far the best thing we eat all night. The cake is an obscenity, a foul, brusque monolith of heavy sponge and cack-handed mousse almost a foot high. It tastes of fat and sugar and disdain. It eats like those showpiece cakes that have sat for years in coffee shop windows look. We are told there is an option to take left-overs home. We choose not to. The last thing we want, as we walk out the door, is to take any part of the dreadful Smith & Wollensky experience with us.

What happened next: This branch of Smith & Wollensky continues to say on its website that it serves 'the best steak in London'. As a later review in The Spectator said, it probably isn't even the best steak in Covent Garden. No matter. Prices remain exactly where they were, and it is still highly rated across customer review sites.

Farm Girl Café
London, 11 March 2018

The menu at the Farm Girl Café features lots of initials. There's V for Vegan. There's GF for Gluten Free. There's DF for Dairy Free. I think they're missing a few. There should be TF for Taste Free and JF for Joy Free and AAHYWEH for Abandon All Hope, Ye Who Enter Here. If you examine the company's website, and I would only advise doing so if you have strong teeth that can cope with a good grinding, you will learn that the Farm Girl group offers: 'A holistic and healthy yet comfortingly simple approach to Australian café culture.' Nope, me neither. Apparently, they like to use 'nutritionally nurturing ingredients', which sounds rather nice. I could have done with a bit of nurture, rather than the dishes that came our way.

I have nothing against eating healthily. I have only one body and I try to look after it. My mother used to say that she hoped to die aged ninety-eight, shot dead by a jealous lover. She didn't quite manage it, but it's an ambition I'm happy to inherit. The menu here is omnivorous with a heavy emphasis on non-meat cookery, which is a fine thing. I like vegetables, me. They can taste really nice. But this sort of cooking does have to be done with skill, grace and, ideally, an absence of malice.

The Farm Girl Café, Chelsea, is the third in a group which until now has stuck to charcoal or matcha lattes, and light lunches involving an awful lot of almond butter, avocado and something called coconut bacon, which you just know isn't. This is the first to serve dinner, and it does indeed look like a proper restaurant in a very Chelsea sort of way. There's a giant blue Welsh dresser behind the bar, faux wooden beams across the ceiling and banquettes in a field shade of green. It's like a cartoon version of a farmhouse as imagined by someone who hasn't been in one.

It fills quickly on a cold winter's evening, with blonde-tressed Chelsea women just bubbling with intolerances. They are fizzing with them, these dairy- and gluten-fearing dietary warriors, seeking sanctuary from the terrifying world of modern food. With them are their pink-cheeked, anxious-looking boyfriends, who clearly fear they are just one more rugby club, traffic-cone-on-your-head piss-up away from being chucked. A woman arrives clutching her Yorkshire terrier. They are given a corner table. The dog is offered a bowl of water and a plate of food and disappears on to the floor for dinner. At least somebody gets to eat well.

From the small plates we order the whole (completely out-of-season) globe artichoke, which apparently is gluten free. It's tough to see how it would be anything other. It has been prepared by someone who either hates globe artichokes or has never met one before: boiled until it is as soft and rank as Grandma's cabbage, only with none of the glamour. It is just so much mushy leaf matter, and smells of a long Sunday afternoon in someone's overheated suburban front room. The damn thing could be disposed of without the aid of teeth or, better still, using a composter. That would remove the middleman, which in this case happens to be me.

'Paola's market veggies' arrive in a bowl, with a grainy, deathly 'carrot hummus' thickly smeared up the side, like someone had an intimate accident and decided to close the loo door and run away. At the bottom is a 'cashew aioli', which is the kind of discharge you get when you torture nuts. It tastes of raw garlic and nothing else. There are sticks of celery and hunks of cauliflower to dredge through this, alongside 'seeded crisp bread' which is neither of the last two words. It is dense and hard and tasteless, as you imagine cork floor tiling might be, if it had somehow been repurposed as food.

Finally, from the small plates, comes tostadas piled with jackfruit, the latest hip, unconvincing replacement for meat. It is a fibrous tangle that gets stuck in your teeth on top of a violent, acidic sludge of guacamole. The jackfruit is described as being barbecued. This means it has been smeared with a blunt barbecue sauce of the kind they serve at pubs with a flat roof. Each of these dishes costs about £8. After this vegan calamity, this extraordinary display of dismal cooking, I find myself eyeing the Yorkshire terrier, greedily. Just hand him over, give me access to the grill, and five minutes.

Perhaps the kitchen can do better with something that once had a pulse. Or perhaps not. The crispy turkey schnitzel sounds nice. Apparently, it is encased in 'lemon and thyme-infused breadcrumbs', but tastes of neither of those things. It barely tastes of anything at all. The meat is overcooked and has the texture of something Timpson's might one day think about using to re-sole my brogues. A heap of pickled cucumber and radish is piled on top helpfully, to ensure the breadcrumbs go soggy. A side dish of roasted cauliflower is so undercooked that the knife barely manages to go through it. The one edible dish is a glutinous, cloyingly sweet vegetable 'curry'. It would be regarded as an utter, shameful travesty by many in south-east Asia, but it's not actively unpleasant.

We do not stay for dessert. They are mostly a list of ice creams and sorbets including a 'spinach, kiwi and coconut oil gelato', which sounds terrifying. What we've ordered so far, plus the second-cheapest bottle of wine, has already run up a bill of just under £100. It's not just the dismal cooking that pains me here. It's the squandering of ingredients and of people's time and the tiresome narrative of 'wellness' with which it's been flogged. I feel especially bad about our waiter. Tom is a good man. He is charming, on point and utterly wasted here; he should do something more socially useful, like fly tipping or nicking cars. I whip out my phone and discover there is a branch of Honest Burgers nearby.

One of their finest, served medium rare, a big heap of rosemary and salt chips and a hefty tumbler of cheap and cheerful sauvignon blanc is exactly what we need to make all those BTGA (Bad Thoughts Go Away).

What happened next: The review received a lot of media attention, especially across Australia. Likewise, Australian commenters below the review online expressed dismay that this should be considered representative of Australian culture. On Facebook the restaurant was asked what they thought of the review. They replied, 'We think it's a very entertaining piece and enjoyed reading it.' The menu has not changed, the Farm Girl Café Chelsea continues to trade and has many positive reviews online.

3

Unlucky Dip

Blue Boar Smokehouse
London, 11 August 2013

Not far from the Blue Boar Smokehouse, which is a
smokehouse much as I am a prima ballerina, is New
Scotland Yard. And so it was that I spent much of lunch
– less eating, more pushing platefuls to one side – wondering whether there were any statutes under which it
would be possible to prosecute the place. Sadly, I concluded that shameless bandwagon jumping, grievous
bodily harm to an entire culinary tradition and atro-
cious cooking are not yet criminal offences. Oh, that
they were. This country would be so much the better
for it. Make me prime minister. I'll sort it.

The Blue Boar Smokehouse is a grotesque marketing
conceit, realised in acres of dark wood veneer, hefty
linen and glassware. It occupies the back room of a
corporate hotel for businessmen, dreaming only of an
in-house movie and a handful of tissues, and feels like
two hours of death by PowerPoint, presented by a life-
style trends consultant who once went to Hoxton. You
can imagine the pitch: 'dirty food' is cool; people like

pulling their pork, whatever that means; fried chicken isn't just for sink estates in Peckham; making this kind of crap is easy and cheap. Fill yer boots.

Or don't. Their ribs arrive dangling out of a mini bucket. Ah yes. I've seen things like this before; it's like experiencing a vicious flashback before you've taken the drugs. The sauce is at first as sharp and acidic as a cheap packet of salt and vinegar crisps and then as sweet as a six-year-old's confection stash. If the meat has spent any time in a smoker, I'm afraid it will take a more acute palate than mine to detect it. My mouth had been brutalised by the sauce. On issues of smoke it had nothing to say.

The least offensive of the main courses is the crab, baked in the shell under a Cajun mayonnaise gunk. It looks like a hefty sneeze into a shell, after a long swim in the sea to clear a cold. To be fair, the first forkful is just about OK. After that it goes from cloying to 'please stop' in easy steps. The accompanying chips would have proved a moment of nostalgia for anybody who has ever worked in a fast food joint emptying the freezer bag into the deep fat fryer.

From the list of pulled meats we order the suckling kid: a heap of something tired and drained, violated and one-note sweet arrives on a wooden board next to glazed onion rolls made from a dough so overworked that tearing them open offers the chance to burn all the calories involved in eating them. The dish is completed by a motorway service station coleslaw.

Worse than this is the 'southern fried chicken', which

must never be granted freedom from within those quotation marks: a tube of breast and a reformed leg, clumsily coated in bright orange crumbs the colour of the cast of *TOWIE*, fried off so limply that those on the bottom come off on the plate. Underneath lies a banana ketchup which has the honour of being the worst thing I have put in my mouth since the incident with the washing-up liquid when I was seven. It tastes like those sweetshop bananas, blitzed with the remains of someone's forgotten 1970s spice cabinet. It looks like something you would treat with antibiotics.

The dessert menu includes an Eton Tidy for £7, which is not merely a violation of ingredients but also of the English language: splodges of strawberry purée, hard, dusty meringue, flaps of crumbly gel, artfully draped. It's the sort of thing that would get a *Professional Master-Chef* contestant sent home in the quarter finals.

As to wines, a waiter had to be called back to deliver a full measure of the glass I had ordered. Shortly, I expect to receive a press release announcing the relaunch of the restaurant at the Intercontinental Hotel, Westminster. I'll regard that as a very good day for London.

What happened next: It took just over a year for the prediction made in the penultimate sentence to be realised. In October 2014 the hotel announced that the restaurant would now be known just as the Blue Boar and that the American BBQ menu was being scrapped to make way for something closer to an English grill menu: lots of smoked salmon, Yorkshire lamb, various steaks, and a pistachio and rhubarb tart to finish. The hotel also changed its name and is now the Conrad London St James, part of the Hilton group.

Star Inn The City
York, 5 October 2014

We all of us have stupid ideas from time to time. We all of us get it wrong. What matters is whether we spot the mistake and make amends. Which is what I told the judge, not that he seemed convinced. Where's mercy when you need it, eh? Happily, I am less ruthless. I'm quick to give credit where it's due. I note, for example, that a restaurant I once reviewed (I say reviewed – I mean butchered, skewered and turned slowly on a spit over guttering flames) has stopped putting peanut butter in with the chicken livers and Marmite in with the potatoes. They have seen the error of their ways. Or at least some of them. Good for them.

Not so, I'm afraid, the Star Inn The City, the £60-a-head York spin-off of chef Andrew Pern's much-lauded Star Inn at Harome in North Yorkshire. When it opened a year ago, so-called rivals in the restaurant-reviewing lark mentioned things about the place that made me flinch and rock to and fro with my eyes closed while calling for Nursie. Knowing I already had negative thoughts without having even been there, I concluded it was better not to review. But then a year passed and I found myself in York with an evening to spare. I feel I should apologise to the restaurant for their bad luck in this regard.

For here it comes, the selection of breads – served in a flat cap, 'cos it's a Yorkshire restaurant, right? And in Yorkshire everything with a pulse wears a flat cap. Always and forever. Yorkshire people slip out of the womb wearing them. Did they buy new flat caps for the purpose? Or were they second-hand? I search the rim for a greasy tide mark. And once you've had the thought you can't help but wonder whose head might have been in your bread basket. It was an absurd and rather unpleasant idea when the restaurant opened – as a number of people said – and it remains so now.

As is a side dish listed as the 'salad o't day'. Look, I enjoy a joke as much as the next anxiety-ridden, sweaty, varicose, misanthropic bastard, but dialect gags like that aren't funny. They're a replacement for things that are funny, made by people who couldn't think of something genuinely funny, and so strained at it like a chap who's been on a low-fibre, high-animal-protein diet for a month.

These two small details – along with the aching wordplay of the establishment's name – go towards making the greater case: that the Star Inn The City is, unfortunately, a really annoying restaurant. It's a crying shame, because God knows York needs reasonable choices. Since the admirable J. Baker's closed, it has been perilously short of them. The conversion of the site, a wide and airy glass vault added to the side of one of York's fine, hulking, ancient buildings, is attractive. And the notion of a good-food pub, coming in out of the countryside like this to the town, is admirable. There's a repertoire of big-knuckled, earthy British-rustic dishes they could have called upon and sometimes they do – but only in name. Then they work them and overwork them, again and again.

Alarm bells start ringing with the menu. It's one of those furiously busy wipe-clean affairs of the sort you'd find in a Brewers Fayre. It has punning section headings complete with exclamation marks, because otherwise you wouldn't know they were being funny. Geddit? So there's 'Good Game, Good Game!' for the game section, because Bruce Forsyth was . . . em, er – no, not a clue. And there's 'On the sauce!' for the list of sauces. I think it's a joke about being drunk. I wish I had been. Plus, it lists every single ingredient, who produced them, where, which direction the wind was blowing from on the day they were harvested. So you get 'cassoulet of Hodgson's of Hartlepool natural smoked haddock', or 'risotto of local estate shot red-legged partridge'. From now on I want to know how every animal on my plate died: 'belly of electrically stunned, throat-slit pork . . .'

The dishes themselves reach for greatness and trip over while doing so. That partridge risotto also contains Wensleydale cheese, chestnuts and kale, but the overwhelming flavour is of truffle oil and demi-glace, that mixture of thickly reduced veal stock with espagnole sauce which makes your lips stick together. If someone had knocked it up from a bit of leftover partridge and a few chestnuts at the back of the fridge you'd be impressed; less so for £10.

Another starter of corned beef is equally disappointing. In recent years corned beef has been saved from the ignominy thrust upon it by Fray Bentos; the modern version can be a beautifully thick, fibrous thing which still resembles a bit of an animal. Here, it arrives in a jelly-topped rectangle with artfully placed pickled silver skin onions scattered hither and yon. None of this can disguise its dull, mushy texture.

A main course of otherwise good roast duck breast is let down by a citrus sausage roll. The filling is too dense, the hit of citrus overwhelming, the pastry undercooked at its heart. But the biggest let-down is the fried fillet of Scarborough woof (Atlantic wolffish), with chip-shop chips and a duck-egg sauce gribiche. If you're going to gussy up what is essentially fish and chips you have to make it better than the original. You have to be playful. This is dense and heavy. I won't call the woof a bit of a dog, even though it is. The fish is dry and fibrous. The chips are the size of my clunking thumbs, and though they taste pleasingly of dripping, are too much claggy potato. Serve these in a chip shop and there would be a riot. At least the sauce gribiche, here essentially a tartar, is a beautiful thing.

Only dessert truly saves honour: a slightly loose but sprightly lemon posset topped with a berry compôte, and a steamed ale cake with a killer butterscotch sauce. Service is fine, if brought to a halt by an attempt to send two other starters we didn't order, compliments of the kitchen, which slowed down the main courses. They were declined. (Note to kitchens: don't do it. Yeah, I know. That we should all have such problems.) Star Inn the City wants to be a culinary guiding light; right now, I'm afraid it's slipping towards being a bit of a black hole.

What happened next: Many York regulars wrote in support of the restaurant, both directly to me and in the online comments section. It rates highly on Open Table and, in 2015, received a very positive review from the Daily Telegraph *which described the food as by turns 'genius' and 'extraordinary', though a review in the* Independent *accused it of playing the Yorkshire card 'with a heavy hand'. I am told they no longer serve bread in flat caps.*

Léon de Bruxelles
London, 22 September 2013

A Friday night and I am sitting in what feels like a dying restaurant. It's not in intensive care yet. Think more high-dependency unit, its owners furiously studying the weekly figures for a settled pulse.

I am in Léon de Bruxelles, the only British outpost of the 120-year-old Belgian mussels-and-chips chain, which has dozens of branches across its home country and France. It's more than three-quarters empty. This is remarkable. Nothing around London's Cambridge

Circus is empty, not on a Friday night. Garfunkel's is full. Café Rouge is full. Despite my very best efforts, the Angus Steakhouse, where they torture steaks nightly, is full.

But not Léon de Bruxelles. You can almost hear the wind blowing between the tables. The transparent laminate covering on the wipe-down mussel-shaped menus is curling off. Then again, why replace them if no one is coming? It can't claim a location problem. It occupies a huge site opposite London's Palace Theatre, is gilded in green bloody neon. Not finding it would require talent. And yet it's all shiny tables and empty seats.

I do find this odd. Mussels in the shell are one of the most gloriously compelling eating experiences there is. They turn the modern eater into ancient hunter-gatherer, roaming the tundra of shiny black shell in search of dinner. Plus, they are a brilliant leveller. However uptight you are, however much of a clean freak, it's impossible to eat them with cutlery. It's a sleeves-up, elbows-on-the-table, get-stuck-in job. Like the flick and pick of the pistachio nut from its shell, the very process of mussel eating is meditative. You zone out and stare deep into the steamy bowl until your eyeballs fog.

Or at least I do. That's why I wanted to go. Long ago I was quite the fan of Belgo, the London-based mussels-and-chips chain where the waiters were all forced to dress like Belgian monks, poor sods. It was serious man-on-mussel action. In 1996 Belgo Centraal, a cavernous and gloomy industrial basement space in Covent Garden which finally brought the aesthetic of a BDSM bar to eating out, was named London restaurant of the year. We were young then. They attempted a brand roll-out, but it didn't take. There are just four left.

And now there's this place which opened last year and which on a Friday night has many staff and few customers. The staff isn't the problem. They are friendly and engaged and have clearly read every page of the training manual, probably a few times. Our waiter almost sounds convincing when he declares their beer cocktails to be 'very special'. The thing is, special ain't the same as good. I knew a chap who could do something 'special' with a lighter and his bodily methane. I wasn't paying for that either. I stick with a good wheat beer.

Part of the problem is the room, which is huge and sterile, with zany things scribbled on brightly coloured boards, the design equivalent of Timmy Mallett's glasses. On closer examination these turn out to be dish names. The room looks like the canteen of a direct marketing company which has tried to inspire the workforce by giving itself a half-arsed makeover. My wife looks around and declares the narcoleptic strawberry blush of the Angus Steakhouse down the road more welcoming. I know how to show a woman a good time.

On one wall there is a photograph of the Manneken Pis; on the other, the silhouette of Tintin. Of course these are not the only famous Belgians. There's a whole board listing 'Les Belges Du Monde' – about a hundred names in total, of which we recognise Jacques

Brel, René Magritte, Brueghel and Johnny Hallyday. There's someone listed as Cockrent, which sounds like the name a male porn star would abandon for destroying all the mystique. On closer examination we identify a full stop between the C and O. We look forward to acquainting ourselves with the work of journalist Christina Ockrent.

We have time to brood on all this because of the aching gaps between courses. There's nothing better guaranteed to make service run slow than a lack of people to serve. If you want to eat quickly, go to a busy restaurant. We watch those who arrived after us being served before us. The food, when it deigns to appear, has OKs and kill-me-now lows. A starter of warm smoked eel, with mustard-smeared toast, is all rich fish oils and kick. It's an expression of the Lowlands, the sort of thing you would eat to ward off chilly fogs. A plate of their charcuterie is a reasonable selection served, predictably, too cold. We let them flog us some slices of dead horse. It is smoked, a little sweet, and rather cloying.

And finally, the mussels. They needed to be good. Being a mussel restaurant that can't do good mussels is like being a cardinal who's crap at praying, or a slaughter man who can't stand the sight of blood. Léon de Bruxelles is all these things and far less. The meat inside the shells is small and shrivelled and dry; each shell contains what looks like the retracted scrotum of a hairless cat. They appear to have been left to steam for too long. Those with Dijon mustard are vinegary. I order the Madras mussels, because it's my stupid job to do so. It's exactly as you would expect Indian food to be were it cooked by Belgians. It smells of old curry-flavoured Pot Noodle; the flavour is not dissimilar. Eating these mussels is not meditative or compelling. It's just disappointing.

The unlimited chips come in deep ceramic pots and are crisp at the top and damp at the bottom where they have steamed in their own heat. Each mussel pot costs a fearsome £14.90. We finish on a high with a freshly made waffle, a crisp puff of malty wonder with whipped vanilla cream, ice cream and maple syrup. I could say I'd come back for that waffle alone, but we all know I wouldn't.

Obviously our meal at Léon de Bruxelles isn't great. That goes without saying. But what really matters is that it's also terribly, terribly sad. That is a failure of a much deeper kind.

What happened next: It was indeed a dying restaurant. A year later, it had closed, to be replaced by a large branch of McDonald's. I'm just so sorry. However, the rest of the Léon de Bruxelles group across Europe – there are ten of them in Paris alone – continue to trade vigorously.

City Social
London, 29 June 2014

You can tell a lot about a place by the punters it attracts. By that measure the City Social, Jason Atherton's new restaurant on the twenty-fourth floor of Tower 42 in the City, is to be avoided, at least by me. Early on I am waiting at the bar where I am approached by a middle-aged woman with hair the colour of the peroxide aisle at Boots. 'I don't normally interrupt people,' she says with the nasal twang of Alison Steadman's Beverly in *Abigail's Party*. 'But I'll make an exception for you. I'm a newly elected UKIP MEP and a real foodie and I'd like to invite you to lunch.'

It speaks much for the Liberal-Left bubble I inhabit that I am astonished she should admit to her UKIP victory. But she's said it with such enthusiasm that it's clear she's said it before and been met with applause. Not this time. 'You support a party which attracts racists, homophobes and bigots,' I say. 'Lunch is not going to happen.' Her lips quiver. 'You're . . . you're the bigot,' she shouts. And she storms off. I suppose in the sense that I am bigoted against bigots I am indeed a bigot, but only over a very narrow bandwidth.

City Social, the latest in a line of London restaurants with the S word in the title, really isn't very. It is all the very worst of the 1980s revisited. It's full of clumping tumours of men, jangling change in their pockets and barking at each other about the latest position taken by Millennium Capital. There are large tables of men, with hard jaws and bald heads and glazed eyes from the working hours, boasting, and stamping and clapping each other on the shoulders. The testicle count is enormously high here, which is fitting because there's an awful lot of bollocks at City Social.

The place is fitted out in the 427 shades of brown visible to the naked eye so as to suggest an old gentlemen's club: curving leather banquettes by the windows, wood trim everywhere, dark floors that suck what available light there is so that menus have to be read by the torch app on your smartphone. Except it's only just opened and has the whiff of the glue-gunned stage set.

They try to serve cocktails in pewter tankards, as if it's a proper old inn that is slipping into the Thames. It isn't. You can tell that from the wraparound view of London up here. It should be said that the chaps behind the bar quickly nod agreement when I laugh in the face of pewter and ask for a bloody glass. Indeed, the barmen are the most human aspect of the whole place.

The rest is faff and bother and heel click. It's the kind of place where dishes are brought on trays by one person but delivered by another in a clumsy dance that stops all conversation; where waiters are drilled to scrape the table for crumbs none can see; where if you decline bread they will remove your bread plate so you may never change your mind. The staff behave as if constantly on the edge of being bawled out by the customers. (Nothing to do with me being recognised; the PR company later made it clear that they didn't know I'd been in.)

Wine service is the pits. It's one of those lists priced to make you feel inadequate. It's priced to give the tedious men barking at each other about Millennium Capital a way to look interesting by spending stupid amounts on wines with names they can't pronounce. I ask the sommelier to find me a bottle of Pinot Noir for under £50. He puffs out his cheeks, shakes his head, points at things costing £56 and, at one point, something costing £99 which isn't Pinot Noir. 'It's very difficult with Pinot Noir,' he says. No it isn't, I tell him. You can get a great one for under a tenner wholesale. It turns out there is one for under £50 – a Chilean for £49 – but I spot it after he has left our table. The man either doesn't know his own list or wants us to spend more.

All this grind and hand wringing and willy-waving makes the food an afterthought, which is a shame. At his best Jason Atherton, who oversees the kitchen here for the consultants Restaurant Associates, which actually runs the venue, can be very good indeed. Witness his seafood linguine: a coil of silky pasta lies in a bowl surrounded by curls of crisped squid, steamed mussels and cockles and a dice of razor clam on the shell. On to this is poured a seafood velouté that is heavy with the cooking juices. Aside from the irritation of wrestling the sauce boat off the waiter so you can have more, it is about as good a seafood pasta dish as you could hope to find in London. As it should be for £14.

But Atherton does have a tendency to overwork things. What might be a great steak tartare – heaps of chopped and seasoned prime beef scattered about the plate – is undermined by splodges of 'dried vinegar', a vinegar gel, the acidity of which bullies the subtleties of the meat. A beautiful tomato salad with tomato jelly and sprinkled with basil granita is let down by tomatoes which are like some of the clientele: all right to look at but with little to say for themselves.

Technically, mains are a masterclass. There are pieces of rabbit saddle, bound together and wrapped in ham to form a cylinder, plus an impressive rabbit sausage and a side dish of a barley-like grain with braised rabbit. A duck dish brings hunks of breast and boulangerie potatoes and a berry compote. Technically impressive they may be, but they lack heart and soul. About the meat there is the raw squidge and bloodiness of sousvide. The animal proteins have been denatured under vacuum, but not uproariously cooked. A kind of perfection has been achieved; it is not the kind I enjoy.

Dessert, at least, is without a fault: a foamy strawberry soufflé, a classic custard tart with a welcome dusting of ground nutmeg. But the whole effect is deadening. Across from Tower 42 is the Heron Tower with, at the top, Duck & Waffle, looking down upon us. Midway through my meal I look up and know that if it's dinner and a view I'm after, that's where I'd rather be. It's twenty floors higher, 50 per cent cheaper and 100 per cent more fun.

What happened next: In Autumn 2014, City Social was named best new restaurant by the website and guide SquareMeal. It went on to be awarded a Michelin star which it has retained year after year. I didn't name the UKIP MEP I got into a row with but it was Janice Atkinson. In March 2015 she was expelled from the party after the Sun *newspaper filmed her allegedly requesting a bill from a restaurant for three times the actual cost of the meal, with the intention of claiming it on expenses.*

The Ten Room
Café Royal, London, 10 February 2013

It was a simple question, and the waiter flunked it. What type of tuna, I asked, do you use in your tartare? I wanted to know if it was endangered bluefin. 'It's from Scotland,' he said, with an authoritative nod of the head. My companions and I looked at each other. Scotland? Why? Was it on holiday there? Had it nipped over from the Pacific to get a job in the oil industry? Later the waiter would return to admit his mistake and tell us it was yellowtail from roughly 8,000 miles to the west of Glasgow. By then it was too late. I already hated the Ten Room at the once-grand Café Royal. In truth I had really started hating it when, just after we sat down, the same waiter offered to recommend something from the menu. He then listed half the dishes, including three of the most expensive starters. So, I asked him, what's wrong with the rest of it? He came out with a special rictus grin, muttered: 'Nothing' and retreated. If you're going to upsell shamelessly, please do it with style.

When they come to hold an inquest into what has gone wrong here – and they surely will, for a deathly echoing space like this cannot afford to be so empty – the kitchen will, for the most part, be found innocent.

The food is not spectacular, but nor is it bad; it's the kind of stuff people who don't look at the bill call comfort food, because it comforts them to eat it.

There's a £12 scallop dish with very little scallop in it. It's amazing how far you can make those suckers go with a sharp knife and a steady hand. There's that tuna tartar and a grilled quail thing with pomegranate to make the kitchen look like it has a bit of Middle Eastern soul. A grilled duck breast for £24 is unevenly cooked: rare as requested at one end, less so at the other – but fine for all that; ditto both a veal chop Holstein, breaded and dressed with a fried egg and anchovies, and a suckling-pig stew. Desserts are better than just OK, especially a warm, soft, spreading chocolate cake and a wobbly custard tart.

The problem is everything else. The space is rather grand – one of those balconied public areas you find in the old art deco hotels of downtown LA. Into it they have plonked a pile of red leather seats and almost nothing else. It's an airline club-class lounge without the design features or the nibbles. Along one side is a wall of square marble posts, backed by glass. The wall looks like a design feature from a self-consciously modernist men's loo. Frankly I didn't know whether to rest upon it or pee against it. By the end I was sorely tempted.

Off to one side, through a doorway, is a bar so dark · you need an iPhone app to read the excruciatingly expensive cocktail list. Music thumps. It continues its muffled thump throughout dinner so that sitting at the table back in the dining area you feel like you're listening to a disco full of young people exchanging rare strains of chlamydia.

Service is silly and pompous and haphazard. I order that suckling-pig stew which, the menu says, comes with crackling. But the crackling doesn't turn up. I have to get the menu back and point it out to the waiter. Don't promise me crackling and then not deliver it.

It's the kind of place where if you decline to have your wine refilled just twice, they'll nick your glass so that you have to ask for it back. Not that you'll be able to afford much to put in it. The cheapest red is £30, and the next cheapest is £40. When the bill comes they ignore the name the booking was made under, presuming they know exactly what I'm doing there, and put my name on it. Only they spell it wrong. And that one detail sums it up. The Ten Room is clumsy, stupid, self-serving and a waste of the once-great Café Royal. It's a crying shame.

What happened next: It was not the happiest of restaurant openings. The Telegraph *called the Ten Room 'dismal', while in* Metro *it was dismissed as a 'sorry, soulless misfire'. However, it traded for five years until, in early 2018, the Café Royal announced it would close and be replaced by a grill and sushi bar under French-born chef Laurent Tourondel, who made his name in New York. Laurent at Café Royal opened in the summer of 2018.*

4

All Fur Coat . . .

Beast
London, 19 October 2014

You could easily respond to this week's restaurant with furious, spittle-flecked rage. You could rant about the posing-pouch stupidity of the meat-hanging cabinet that greets you as the lift doors open, and the frothing tanks of monstrous live Norwegian king crabs next to it, each 4ft across. You could bang on about the bizarre pricing structure, and the vertiginous nature of those prices; about the rough-hewn communal tables that are so wide you can't sit opposite your dining companion because you wouldn't be able to hear each other, and the long benches which make wearing a skirt a dodgy idea unless you're desperate to flash the rest of the heavily male clientele. You could shake your fists and roll your eyes and still not be done.

I think this would be a mistake. Instead you should accept Beast as the most unintentionally funny restaurant to open in London in a very long time. It's hilariously silly. The most appropriate response is to point and laugh. I don't even think I'd advise you not to go.

As long as you go with someone else's money, because God knows you'll need a lot of it. Got any friends who are, say, international drug barons? Excellent. They may be able to afford dinner. It's worth going to see what the unmitigated male ego looks like, when expressed as a restaurant.

If Beast were a chap, he would be a part-time rugby player smelling of Ralgex who's trying to tell you he's deep and thoughtful, even though he'll later be implicated in an incident involving a traffic cone and a pint glass of his own urine. It is a venture by the Moscow-born company behind the admirable steakhouse Goodman, and the clever and ever-expanding chain Burger and Lobster, where you can get only an expensive burger or a cheap lobster, both for £20. Beast is essentially a luxe version of the latter.

When it first opened a few months ago, it offered only a set menu for £75 a head: a few antipasti of aged Parmesan and the like, followed by 400g of bone-in rib-eye per person, and a quarter each of Norwegian king crab, a species which cleverly manages to be both a delicacy and a cause for concern to environmentalists due to the way it is advancing down the Norwegian coast. This is to be eaten at those huge 6ft-wide communal tables, planted with guttering candelabras. There are dry-stone walls and glass-fronted wine cabinets bulging with Montrachet and Pomerol, priced in four figures for men with teeny-weeny penises. I order one of the very cheapest options, a Bordeaux by the glass.

A few days before our booking, Beast had introduced

an à la carte option. Apparently not everyone wanted the full Beasting. Given the apparent intention to make everything more relaxed, the pricing system is utterly dysfunctional. The starters, priced in the mid-teens, are the best value. Thick slices of impeccable yellowfin tuna, seared and then chilled, come with an insistent lemon aïoli. Even better are the grilled red prawns, offering huge head-suckage possibilities.

We watch the salty juices pool on the plate, exploding with umami, and conclude we need bread. 'I'm sorry sir, we don't serve bread.' Eh? What's all that about? I could see this as some stand for a bang-on-trend, carb-free Palaeolithic diet, were it not for the fact they serve chips. Mind you, they're crap chips, huge fat things that could exclude draughts. Who actually likes their chips this way? They're advertised as coming with truffle and foie-gras salt, which is like getting a gold-plated, diamond-encrusted case for your smartphone because you've run out of things to spend money on. It's a spoilt person's version of luxury; the pillowy 'chips' do not taste either of goose liver or truffle.

Next, we want a single serving of the rib-eye – 400g – and a single serving of the crab. This is where it all collapses. The beef is listed at £10 per 100g. But the smallest cut they have is 600g. You're in for £60. With the crab, which costs £75 a kilo, it's even sillier. You have to buy a whole beast, and the smallest they have is 4.3kg, at a mere £325.50. Before service. We have to make do with a single spindly leg at £25. It's served with a cloyingly sweet basil and chilli dressing which makes us bare our teeth. Of course, despite the price, you have to extract the meat from the shell yourself using scissors, picks, crackers and a heart monitor. It's a messy business for not very much sweet meat. I ask for a finger bowl. They don't do those either. I am directed to the hard stone sinks around the edges. Maybe I should save on a walk to the men's while I'm there. It feels like that sort of place.

The corn-fed, dry-aged Nebraskan rib-eye, with a carbon footprint big enough to make a climate-change denier horny, is bloody marvellous: rich, deep, earthy, with that dense tang that comes with proper hanging. And at £100 a kilo it bloody well should be. At that price they should lead the damn animal into the restaurant and install it under the table so it can pleasure me while I eat. We love the buttery truffle sauce that comes with it. We love the bone, which demands to be taken in hand. We especially love a side salad of plump multicoloured tomatoes in a smoky dressing.

At the end there is a lemon mousse which is too much acidity and nowhere near enough fruit. There is also a 'deconstructed' vanilla cheesecake, which, as too often, is code for: 'We couldn't be bothered to make a proper cheesecake.' A cushion of whipped vanilla cream lies under a landslide of shattered digestives with a few berries in mourning. And all of this is served with huge solemnity and seriousness. It may be hilarious, but those involved have no idea. It is also full of men, being manly. Looking around I finally conclude that Beast is the sort of restaurant invented solely to be photographed for in-flight magazines determined to present a portrait of your home city you do not recognise. I imagine there will soon be one in New York which will look just like this, with Dubai close behind and Moscow after that. They will all look the same. They will all cost the earth. They will all be completely and utterly absurd.

What happened next: This was a masterclass in how a restaurant should respond to a less than positive review. That morning Dave Strauss, the general manager for the group that includes Beast, tweeted out that 'fellating cows' were en route to the restaurant to satisfy my needs. He told me later that the phone was soon ringing off the hook that day, with people wanting to see what I had described for themselves. He and I became firm friends, and I became a regular at another of the group's restaurants, Zelman Meats in Soho. Today, the menu is a more standard affair, with various steak cuts available by the 100g, and king crab at £120 per kilo. They do now serve bread. They are hoping to open a Miami franchise of Beast in 2019.

Dorchester Grill
The Dorchester, London, 28 December 2014

Of all the dirty food acts I have committed – that dribbling sausage I ate from the late-night cart in Leicester Square, a solo dinner at Frankie and Benny's, a Greggs pasty which I quietly enjoyed – this feels like the very worst. I am going for dinner in an establishment I am meant to be boycotting. Recently the Sultan of Brunei introduced sharia law, including the stoning to death of homosexuals. As he owns the Dorchester Hotel, I should not be darkening its door. But I've always believed that the best way to deal with bigotry is to laugh in its face. And oh my, is there a lot to laugh at about the Dorchester. And it's not just the women in the mink bomber jackets with the face lifts so tight the classic Brazilian risks becoming a Van Dyke beard.

What's most amusing is that of all the great London hotels, the Dorchester has always been the campest. The wide corridor of a lobby is a riot of soft furnishings and tassels and cushions so plump you could fake a pregnancy with them. It is a masterclass in try-too-hard fabulous. For many years the counterfeit jewel in this paste crown was the Dorchester Grill, a room off to the side where the walls were decorated with 12ft murals of big-thighed chaps in kilts tossing things hither and yon. The carpet was a massive tartan print and the banquettes were studded lumps of red brocade. Stereotyping queer culture as one thing or another is almost as stupid as trying to ban it. But let's just say it was ironic for an apparently homophobic sultan to own a room like this.

For years talented chefs came and went from here, knocking out smart dishes that simply couldn't compete with the walls. It didn't matter what those poor cooks did. Everyone came out muttering about the kilts. So now Alain Ducasse (who already runs the dour Michelin three-star down the hall) has taken control, and the room has had a makeover. And yes, the murals have gone. But oh my! What they've put in their place! It takes an awful lot of money to make a room look this cheap. It's a space that hasn't been allowed to hear the words: 'That will do.' It's all mirrors and gilding and desperation. The caramel-coloured leather banquettes even have broad fold-down armrests of the sort you'd find in a Mercedes S Class, so you don't have to touch your companion. It looks like the inside of a little girl's plastic music box.

To view all this, you must first negotiate the sharp-creased and -heeled automatons on the desk in the corridor outside who find our request to wait at the bar difficult to comprehend. It turns out you have to ask just the three times. Through the doors and we are confronted by a wall stacked with five figures' worth of shiny, pink-tinted copperware. A couple of shelves are taken up with jelly moulds, and it is those which sums up what's going on here. There may be battalions of impeccably French staff both front and back of house doing their best to patronise the hell out of you. But when you drill down on the menu it's what the faded gentry used to call high tea. It's nursery food at stupid prices. Come on, Nanny: safety-pin my XXXL nappy in place and bring me din-dins.

You can call breaded fingers of lemon sole 'goujo-nettes' if you really like, but that doesn't stop them looking like something out of a freezer bag from Iceland, and it certainly doesn't justify a £17 price tag. As for the rest, there's no doubting the technique. There are people in that kitchen who doubtless could recite pages of *Larousse Gastronomique* at you like it was the litany. But all that technique is then pressed into the service of the dull and lifeless. A puck of cheese soufflé in a cheese sauce has a fine, soft texture, but eats like a dish you would get spooned into your mouth by some-one else when you're feeling poorly.

A lobster bisque makes its point through udder-squirts of cream. Pâté en croûte is a dense cramming-to-gether of blitzed animal between two slivers of pressed pastry, all served far too cold. Main courses are prime ingredients at excruciating prices. A beef fillet for £46 comes with a Yorkshire pudding which isn't as good as those I make, alongside a dry bit of sawn-through marrowbone topped with breadcrumbs. Most odd is two slices of pork belly, cooked for seven hours before being grilled, in a sticky glaze that smells lightly of Marmite. The fat yields, but the meat is hard, which is a remarkable achievement for something that's appar-ently been cooked for so long. A veal chop escapes with its virtue.

If there's a point to coming here it's dessert – espe-cially a pistachio soufflé with a liquid salted-caramel centre from its 'soufflé list'. But again, while I can admire the technique I can't admire the £14 price tag. Worryingly, lemon tart is described as being made 'our way', which predictably means it's not a tart at all but a dome of meringue filled with lemon curd. If only they would do it someone else's way.

Thank God for the company I kept that night, for there is something utterly joyless about this place. It's that killer combination of smugness and dreariness;

it's the restaurant equivalent of the office bore. Often I'm asked why I bother visiting restaurants like this where the bill swiftly reaches enough to buy the cuff on a mink bomber jacket. Partly it's rubbernecking. I do love watching the oblivious rich in surroundings of acute bad taste masquerading as good. But it's also that these restaurants attempt to fool people into thinking they are worth it if only they could save up. It's useful to know that they are not.

So yes, you can hate the Dorchester Grill on principle. You can avoid the whole damn hotel on the grounds that its knuckle-dragging owner thinks stoning strangers to death is a reasonable response to their sexual orientation. But I think it helps to know that you can also hate it on its own terms; that the price tag will not buy you bliss or, as the best restaurants do, a moment suspended in time. It will simply buy you the sense that some people have too much money and others know how to take it off them.

What happened next: In 2017 the grill was included in the 'Top 50 Best Restaurants in London' as compiled by reservation service Bookatable. The menu is still fiercely expensive but has been rewritten into plain English so no longer includes 'goujonettes' or 'pâté en croûte'. Most disappointingly vegetables 'of the moment' have been replaced by vegetables which are merely 'seasonal'. While it does not have a star, it is included in the Michelin guide.

The Rib Room
The Jumeirah Carlton Tower Hotel, London,
4 December 2011

At the Rib Room you are never alone. It doesn't matter whether you might wish to be; whether you thought you might have a quiet, relatively uninterrupted chat over dinner with your companion. The waiters will still come at you in waves, fiddling with glassware, fidgeting with bread, asking you how everything is.

'Not sure, mate,' I wanted to shout. 'Every time I'm about to taste something you come up and ask how everything is.' Not that they are completely unhelpful. Having asked to be moved from an over-lit table in the middle of the room to a corner banquette, we were handed one of those flashlights on a flexible stem for reading books by. 'We find this is a rather dark corner,' the waiter said, 'so we thought this might help.' He wasn't wrong. This is the first time I have found myself in a space so dark that I literally needed a torch to read the menu.

It read well. Sadly, reading well was pretty much all it did, which was a disappointment. Eating at the Rib Room at the Carlton Tower Hotel is a Knightsbridge tradition, much like money-laundering and Botox. When the hotel opened exactly fifty years ago it was the tallest in London and the oak bar with granite inlay in the restaurant was the place to be seen. It has a reputation for being a little bit flash and a little bit louche but for trading in the most basic of virtues: prawn cocktails, ribs of Aberdeen Angus beef and so on.

Back in 1961 it described itself as offering: 'A gourmet's feast in an atmosphere of masculine hearty good cheer,' which makes it sound like a rugby club changing room.

I'm not sure much has changed. Today it's the kind of place where chaps with broad necks and suits that shimmer under the down lighters talk softly of the old days in Odessa before they all struck it rich.

And rich they must be for, famously, the prices are brutal. Recently the Rib Room went through a make-over, to give it a new interior in shades of green and amber, and a new chef with experience at Northcote Manor in Lancashire. The website now talks about his commitment to local produce which is all very now and all very silly in this corner of London, unless they really are digging up carrots from Battersea Park. Or shooting the ducks on the scum-laden boating ponds. Which they aren't. In any case it probably is best to get the scallops from Orkney rather than, say, the Thames down from Bermondsey.

The scallops, a plural apparently achieved by the slicing of one large one into three, came nicely seared, and laid on what was described as apple-glazed bacon, but was instead something half an inch thick and soft and braised and an insult both to the word bacon and to the pig. At £16 we expected more. A lot more. By comparison the thickly piled Rib Room prawn cocktail for the same price almost felt like good value (though only if you did happen to get lucky in the botched nationalisation of Russian public utilities all those years ago).

The famed Rib of Beef, an inch-thick hunk of

Aberdeen Angus served with gravy and a Yorkshire pudding, is listed online as costing £40. Get to the Rib Room itself and suddenly it's £42. Why is it never the other way round? There are lots of jokes I could make here about how, for that price, you'd want the animal to come out and give you a dance and a joke, perhaps a tour of the new dining room. But, actually, I'd have happily settled for it tasting nice. In the sixties the Rib Room declared their ambition to serve the best beef in London. Today I'm not even sure it's the best beef on Cadogan Place.

The meat was completely under-seasoned and was so much dull, wet cotton wool. I left at least fifteen quid's worth of it on the side of my plate, because I simply couldn't be fagged to carry on dragging it through my teeth. The gravy was like an episode of *Downton Abbey*: it looked all right but had absolutely no depth. The Yorkshire had the texture of something that had been loitering in the kitchen for a while.

Generally, I have little time for people who say they could have made a restaurant dish at home; eating out is about so much more than whether you can be fagged to cook or not. But I really can make this so much better at home – and at a quarter of the price. Or make that a fifth of the price, for side dishes – a thin cauliflower cheese, a more pleasing bowl of spinach with shallots – are £4.50 each, or just over a fiver if you chuck in the obligatory 12.5 per cent service. Funnily enough online they are listed at £4. Sorry to bang on about this but, given they have literally just re-launched, the under-pricing online feels like a conveniently sloppy mistake.

A more complex duck dish – a bit of breast, a braised and re-formed leg, some figs – was exactly the same. It was a big plate of blah, an essay on the finer points of dull and, in the darkness of our corner, didn't even have looks going for it. 'If they'd put as much effort into the food as they do at hounding us with waiters it might have been a good meal,' said my companion. She had a point.

The best part of our dinner was a light, wobbly apple-crumble soufflé, which lived up to its title. Far less appealing was a martini glass layered with an (over-) set cream of white chocolate and cardamom, and a coffee and whisky jelly, all of it beneath a thick layer of milk foam. The latter was the stuff of so many adolescent school-boy jokes that aren't even worth making.

The 500-strong wine list is priced to keep the hoi polloi out and succeeds. There is, it should be said, a cheaper lunchtime menu at £25 for three courses, but for that you get not rib but braised heel of beef, a cut so lowly even the shin looks down upon it.

I am minded to say that after a few weeks of eating outside the capital this is the sort of thing which gives London dining a very bad name and that they wouldn't get away with it outside the M25. But, actually, I don't think they'd get away with it outside SW1. They charge like this for such lacklustre food because they know their clientele don't really care about either cost or quality. And it really shows.

Throughout the meal the waiters insisted on addressing me rather ostentatiously by the pseudonym I had used when booking. 'Yes Mr—', 'No Mr—', 'Here's your dessert Mr—'. They did it so much and with such conviction that I began to wonder whether, refreshingly, I actually hadn't been rumbled. No chance. I was in a cab on my way home and looking at my Twitter feed – a filthy habit, I know – when I noticed a tweet from the Rib Room thanking me for dining with them that evening. Amazing. I was a mile away from the place, and I still couldn't get rid of the bloody waiters.

What happened next: Apparently not very much, because the roast rib of beef is still £42, a remarkable lack of price movement over seven years since the review. In 2017 it was announced that chef Tom Kerridge of the Hand and Flowers in Marlow would be taking over the Rib Room; however Kerridge pulled out of the deal a few months later in favour of the Corinthia Hotel near London's Trafalgar Square. The Rib Room continues to operate much as it did in 2011 and has generally positive ratings from online reviewers.

Quattro Passi
London, 7 September 2014

In the closing years of her life my late mother, who once loved restaurants, came to despair of them. Her hearing was failing and the spaces that were once ideal for banter and gossip became the enemies of such. Restaurants, it transpired, are mostly designed by young people with no understanding of acoustics; who think hard surfaces and polished concrete are easy on the eye, regardless of how cruel they are to the ear. The crash and clatter of self-regarding modern restaurant design managed what almost no one and nothing else could: they rendered my mother silent.

September 9 marks the start of Lipreading Awareness Week, and they asked that I consider the impact of design on those who are hard of hearing. I'm more than willing to oblige. What's wrong with a bit of carpet? And maybe the odd curtain? A low ceiling and a bit of enclosed booth seating wouldn't go amiss either. I hate the fact that some people are missing my wittiest lines over dinner simply because of crap design.

And so I decided to book a restaurant that I was sure would be acoustically sympathetic. Actually, I needed one, because the fates have a cruel sense of humour. I had returned from my summer holidays with both a glorious tan and a less-glorious ear infection. I was genuinely hard of hearing. I fell upon the newly opened Quattro Passi in Mayfair. The original on the Amalfi coast has two Michelin stars. Now chef Antonio Mellino has apparently moved it here to 'introduce Londoners to real Italian fine dining'. Charmed, I'm sure. The website talked of leather wall finishes and French silk wallpaper and a chandelier made from thousands of tiny silk petals. It bellowed softness. Perfect.

Except it isn't. It's all hard floors and hard walls and high ceilings. Happily, there was no sound system. Until we sat down. Then they cranked it up right over our heads. We were the only people there that lunch-time. I shouted to the waitress to please, in the name of all that is holy, turn it off.

She shouted back: 'What?'

Well, exactly. Eventually we convinced them to return us to a hard, echoing silence. Still, I cannot recommend Quattro Passi to the hard of hearing. Happily, on this occasion they need not feel excluded, because I cannot recommend Quattro Passi to anybody. Few restaurants have left me feeling so angry, and it has nothing to do with the acoustics. Because few restaurants sum up the shameless, disfigured, toxic economics currently at work in certain central London postcodes as much as this one. It is a business seemingly designed to milk a luxe economy that values pointless fripperies over real value. It is an insult to good taste in three courses.

We drank one glass of sparkling wine each (not champagne) and one glass of white and ran up a bill of £282. I could find no bottle of wine on the list for less than £40. After that you need oxygen to read the prices, which top out in five figures. Antipasti and pasta dishes are between £20 and £34. Main courses are almost all £40, with some more than that. I tried to imagine the meeting where they priced a bowl of poorly roasted new potatoes – oily, sweaty, soft-skinned, as though cooked a while before and then reheated to order – at £6. Did they urge each other ever higher, giggling as they calculated the enormous gross profit?

I've said it many times: I have no problem spending big money on meals out. I've paid more than £282 of my own dosh for lunch. It just needs to be utterly memorable, the stuff of recollections whispered breathily late at night. It can't be a pallid fart of mediocrity, priced for some dodgy clientele that's ripped off the gross national product of a small impoverished nation and is now domiciled in London for tax reasons. That's what your money gets you at Quattro Passi: clumsy cooking, trying to make itself look grown up and clever, generally by the application of flaky precious metals, like King Midas has suffered psoriasis over your dinner. Yes, really. We'll get there.

Of course, a kitchen at this level can do basic things. They can make good breads. They can grill a bit of fish. They can make a pistachio ice cream. But none of that is good enough, not for £282. An amuse-bouche brings a stodgy croquette, the size and colour of a cat's turd, on a thick tomato purée full of metallic tang. Apparently the brown item is made of aubergine; I'm grateful for the heads up or I wouldn't have known. It is a dull vegetal thud. The seafood risotto costs £34. At that price it should be the best I have ever eaten, Neptune's-tears-made-lunch. This is a dense salty pond, with little in the way of the iodine tang seafood lovers crave. The shellfish has been diced up so finely that it is undiscoverable amid the soupy rice, because obviously rich people don't like chewing. The fact that it is flecked with silver leaf does not make it better. Does it make it better for anybody? Who swoons over such things?

Ravioli of smoked cheese, costing £20, is an adequate plate of pasta of the sort you could get at any reasonable trattoria. Ditto the £48 grilled fish. Well done. You bought some fish and you grilled it. A plate of lamb medallions, ordered medium rare but served medium and dry, is a whole bunch of bad ideas. There are skid marks of bitter chocolate that have dried on to the plate. There is a bizarre dehydrated raspberry crumble. There are fresh raspberries. Lamb and raspberries have been introduced to each other. They never need meet again. This is a truly awful piece of cooking.

A strawberry tiramisu is not a tiramisu at all. It's an odd, sickly, coffee-free cream affair with a jammy centre, in a collar of over-thick white chocolate. For £12 you'd think they'd remove the green foliage from the strawberries, but no. Still, there's gold leaf; paging a dermatologist for Mr Midas. It's a dessert as designed by an eight-year-old girl who's been given a new pack of colouring pens.

I could bang on but, oh God, they've turned up the music again. I cannot hear my companion, but I can hear myself think. My thoughts are ugly. And so to the old gag. The best part about lunch at Quattro Passi? Leaving.

What happened next: Quattro Passi closed in 2017.

Le Cinq
Four Seasons Hotel George V, Paris, 9 April 2017

There is only one thing worse than being served a terrible meal: being served a terrible meal by earnest waiters who have no idea just how awful the things they are doing to you are. And so, to the flagship Michelin three-star restaurant of the George V Hotel in Paris, or the scene of the crime as I now like to call it. In terms of value for money and expectation Le Cinq supplied by far the worst restaurant experience I have endured in my eighteen years in this job. This, it must be said, is an achievement of sorts.

It wasn't meant to be so. Irritated by reader complaints about the cost of eating out I decided to visit a classic Parisian gastro-palace, as a reality check. I imagined it less as review, and more as an observational piece, full of moments of joy and bliss, of the sort only stupid amounts of cash can buy. We'd all have a good laugh at rich people and then return to business as usual, a little wiser. I chose Le Cinq, restaurant of Christian Le Squer, named chef of the year by his peers in 2016. I assumed it would be whimsical, and perhaps outrageous. Never did I think the shamefully terrible cooking would slacken my jaw from the rest of my head.

The dining room, deep in the hotel, is a broad space of high ceilings and coving, with thick carpets to muffle the screams. It is decorated in various shades of taupe, biscuit and fuck you. There's a little gilt here and there, to remind us that this is a room designed for people for whom guilt is unfamiliar. It shouts money much as football fans shout at the ref. There's a stool for the lady's handbag. Well, of course there is.

Menus the height of Richard Osman are brought. My female companion, who booked the table, is given one without prices. Waiters look baffled when we protest but replace it. Then again, having looked at those prices I suspect many people would wish never to see their like again. Starters and mains are roughly the same price, running from €70 to €140. Currently the exchange rate is 0.86 to 1. So that's £121 for a single plate of food.

All this comes with canapés and amuse-bouches, pre-desserts and bread and serious attitude. Almost all the pleasant things we eat come from the pastry section. There's a compelling flaky brioche, to be eaten with cool, salty butter. There is, among the canapés, a tart of extremely thin pastry with a filling of whipped chicken liver mousse topped by diced cornichon. I could eat that again. At the end there are some pleasant enough chocolates. At these prices there should be.

Other things are the stuff of therapy. The canapé we are instructed to eat first is a transparent ball on a spoon. It looks like a Barbie-sized silicone breast implant, and is a 'spherification', a gel globe using a technique perfected by Ferran Adrià at El Bulli about twenty years ago. This one pops in our mouth to release stale air with a tinge of ginger. My companion winces. 'It's like eating a condom that's been left lying about in a dusty greengrocer's,' she says. Spherifications of various kinds – bursting, popping, deflating, always ill-advised – turn up on many dishes. It's their trick, their shtick, their big idea. It's all they have. Another canapé, tuile enclosing scallop mush, introduces us to the kitchen's love of acidity. Not bright, light aromatic acidity of the sort provided by, say, yuzu. This is blunt acidity of the sort that polishes up dulled brass coins.

We hit it again in an amuse-bouche which doesn't: a halved and refilled passionfruit, the vicious passionfruit supplemented by a watercress purée that tastes only of the plant's most bitter tones. My lips purse, like a cat's arse that's brushed against nettles.

The cheapest of the starters is gratinated onions 'in the Parisian style'. We're told it has the flavour of French onion soup. It makes us yearn for a bowl of French onion soup. It is mostly black, like nightmares, and sticky, like the floor at a teenager's party. There are textures of onions, but what sticks out are burnt tones, and spherified balls of onion purée that burst jarringly against the roof of the mouth. A dish of raw marinated scallops with sea urchin ice cream is a whack of iodine. It is the most innovative dish of the meal, though hardly revolutionary. Sea urchin ice cream turned up on *Iron Chef America* back in the noughties.

A main of pigeon is requested medium but served so pink it just might fly again given a few volts. It comes with brutally acidic Japanese pear and more of that flavourless watercress purée. A heap of couscous is mined with a tiny portion of lamb for €95. Like the watercress purée, it tastes of little. It comes with gummy purées, unpleasant spherifications of lamb stock and mushy, one-note 'merguez' sausages which are nothing of the sort. A sad, over-reduced sauce coagulates on the plate.

A dessert of frozen chocolate mousse cigars wrapped in tuile is fine, if you overlook the elastic flap of milk skin draped over it, like something that's fallen off a burns victim. A cheesecake with lumps of frozen parsley powder is not fine. I ask the waitress what the green stuff is. She tells me and says brightly: 'Isn't it great!' No,

I say. It's one of the worst things I've ever eaten. It tastes of grass clippings. Parsley is brilliant with fish. But in cheesecake? They take it off the bill. With our mint tea, we are served an on-trend kouign amann, a laminated caramelised pastry. It's burnt around the edges.

With this, we each drink one glass of champagne, one glass of white and one of red, chosen for us by the sommelier from a wine list that includes bottles at €15,000. The booze bill is €170. The overall bill is €600. Every single thing I ate at the restaurant Skosh for a sixth of the price was better than this. It's bizarre. Not that the older gentlemen with their nieces on the few other occupied tables seem to care. The restaurant is never more than half full. Pictures of plates are snapped. Mind you I also take pictures, but mine are shot in the manner of a scene of crime officer working methodically.

I have spent sums like this on restaurant experiences before and have not begrudged it. We each of us build our best memories in different ways, and some of mine involve expensive restaurants. But they have to be good. This one will also leave me with memories. They are bleak and troubling. If I work hard, one day, with luck, I may be able to forget.

What happened next: Apart from a bit of media noise, not a whole lot. Le Cinq still has three Michelin stars. Christian Le Squer is still the head chef. Indeed, there appears to be only one major change: the nine-course tasting menu has risen in price from €310 to €340.